Justice for Raymond

Justice for Raymond

Raymond McCord

Gill & Macmillan

Gill & Macmillan Ltd
Hume Avenue, Park West, Dublin 12
with associated companies throughout the world
www.gillmacmillan.ie

© Raymond McCord 2008
978 07171 4414 3

Typography design by Make Communication
Print origination by TypeIT, Dublin
Printed by ColourBooks Ltd, Dublin

This book is typeset in Minion 12 on 15.

The paper used in this book comes from the wood pulp of
managed forests. For every tree felled, at least one tree is planted,
thereby renewing natural resources.

A CIP catalogue record for this book is available from the British
Library.

5 4 3 2 1

*This book is dedicated
to the memory of our son Raymond Jnr
and to the good people of our country*

Contents

FOREWORD BY NUALA O'LOAN   IX

PREFACE   XI

ACKNOWLEDGMENTS   XV

1.   A Hard Man is Born   1

2.   Your Head's for Thinking, Your Fists for Fighting   10

3.   Paramilitaries were Not for Me   19

4.   Sandsy, Me and Star of the Sea   28

5.   The Shipyard and the Foundry   37

6.   Young Raymond is Born   46

7.   We've Found your Son's Body Murdered   55

8.   The Hunt for Raymond's Killers   78

9.   Mount Vernon UVF Unmasked   100

10.   Operation Ballast   125

11.   At Last I am Finally Vindicated   149

12.   From Agent Helen to Agent Roxy   170

13.   Hitting the Election Trail   194

14.   Washington Hears My Story   206

Foreword

Raymond McCord is a brave man. His son was murdered in 1997 and since then he has fought a long and lonely battle in what must, on occasion, have been terrifying times, to try to bring 'young Raymond's' murderers to justice. The story he told me in 2002, when he walked into my office in Belfast, was chilling — a story of men involved in murder, arson, extortion, armed robbery, intimidation and many other crimes, who were, he told me, effectively above the law, men who were protected because they were police informants. His was a compelling and terrible allegation. I was determined that we would conduct an independent impartial investigation. It took over four years.

In January 2007 I reported my findings: a police informant, whom I did not and cannot name, was among the identifiable suspects for the murder; there were failures in the murder investigation and this one individual was implicated by intelligence in at least ten murders, ten attempted murders and seventy-two other crimes over a twelve-year period.

This story would never have been told had Raymond McCord not persisted in his fight for justice.

Nuala O'Loan
February 2008

Preface

Murderers, drug dealers, extortionists, knee-cappers, bombers: all in the pay of Her Majesty's Government. Not fiction, but the truth that was uncovered by the Police Ombudsman for Northern Ireland, Nuala O'Loan. Her investigation 'Operation Ballast' was the most damning report relating to police cover-ups and collusion with the UVF to come out of her office.

It covered at least ten murders, ten attempted murders, punishment shootings, drug dealing, criminal damage, extortion and intimidation, all carried out by a unit of the UVF from Mount Vernon and Newtownabbey. The result was sickening for both the victims and their families, because no one was charged with those crimes, thanks to corrupt practices by officers in the Special Branch.

The UVF unit was headed up by Mark Haddock who had been recruited as an informant while in his teens by the Criminal Investigation Department. Eventually the Special Branch took over as his handlers. While working for the Branch he was said to have been involved in at least ten murders and other serious crimes, yet he was paid a minimum of £80,000 by the State even though the Special Branch knew what he was doing. Instead of helping to prevent murders and other terrorist acts, Haddock was personally involved in a number of murders and was the guiding hand for other assassination squads. He had a terrible reputation for violence within his community; nobody in Mount Vernon dared to challenge him. Those who tried were either murdered or severely beaten. Haddock thought no one could stop him.

One man did.

Haddock's downfall was the murder of Raymond McCord Jnr when I, as his father, decided to get to the truth of his murder. What I was to learn about Haddock, about the UVF whose leader was also working as an informant, and about the Special Branch, was simply unbelievable. Yet it was the truth.

I had made a promise to my son as he lay in the funeral parlour. I reached into the coffin and held his hand. I told him that I would personally hunt down the killers and expose them. It was a promise I would keep.

For five years after the murder, I conducted a one-man campaign for justice for Raymond Jnr, and then decided to seek the help of Nuala O'Loan. I had to. None of the Unionist politicians had lived up to their promises to help me in my quest for justice. Mrs O'Loan was my last hope.

Her investigation was hampered by the lack of co-operation of some senior police officers, past and present. Other problems arose due to funding. But all were overcome thanks to the tenacity of Mrs O'Loan and her team of dedicated investigators. The bottom line was that the Special Branch was a force within a force, a force which 'babysat' interviews with murderers so as to ensure that they did not admit to murder — because of course they were working *for* Special Branch!

The Special Branch also provided the Director of Public Prosecutions with misleading statements and information to protect informants. The 'bigger picture' was the Special Branch's reason. No one could be charged without their authorisation. No house could be searched without their giving clearance, for fear that guns, explosives or drugs might be found inside an informant's house.

All of this would have stayed within the corridors and hidden files of the Special Branch, had not the Police Ombudsman shone a light into its darkest and murkiest secrets.

And had I not walked into Nuala O'Loan's office, her investigators would not have had the opportunity to open up such a can of worms.

This is the story of how I helped to rock the British establishment to the core and expose what many had believed before: that Northern Ireland was involved in a dirty war between police and terrorist groups; that this had resulted in many innocent people paying the ultimate price with their lives; and that collusion between security forces and terrorists in murders was a major factor in many cases. This was Northern Ireland, where life meant nothing to the faceless people who controlled the security forces. Murder didn't matter.

One father decided that his son's murder wouldn't be just another statistic, and fought the system. This is my story.

Raymond McCord
April 2008

Acknowledgments

I would like to pay special thanks to John Cassidy for helping me not only with the book, but also for keeping Raymond's case in the public eye.

In my family, Vivienne, Gareth and Glenn showed great patience with me and gave me strength.

There are very many to thank in the media: Chris Hagan, Chris Thornton, David Gordon and Stephen Breen, to name a few.

My solicitor Paul Farrell was at first just a solicitor, but became a personal friend.

Thanks to Jane Winters for her support, and to Frank McNeill, Tommy Benson, the late John Niblock, Seamus, Roy, wee Jim (Mr O), Jackie, Johnny, Terry and Kenny, friends who stood by me.

Thanks to Lady Sylvia Hermon and Darwin Templeton.

To my mum, I love you.

To Nuala O'Loan and her office, we showed them!

I thank Fergal Tobin for giving me the chance to tell the true story of collusion and the murder of a much loved son. I hope I've done Raymond proud.

1.
A Hard Man is Born

Growing up in the largest housing estate in western Europe at the start of the Troubles was particularly hard. With no older brothers to fight my battles, I learned quickly to use my hands and feet. This was life in the school of hard knocks where young boys quickly grew up to be men.

I was born Raymond Irvine McCord on 23 December 1953, the second child of Kathleen and Hector McCord. My sister Jean was seven years older. My mum gave birth to me in the Royal Maternity Hospital in Belfast. While she nursed me, my dad was out 'wetting my head' with a few pints with his Catholic friend Jimmy Saunders from the New Lodge Road area of north Belfast. It is difficult for many people today to understand that my dad, who was a member of the Orange Order, the Royal Black Preceptory and the Apprentice Boys of Derry, would be drinking and celebrating the birth of his only son with a Catholic. But that was Belfast before the Troubles started. Jimmy and my dad threw darts together in the Gem bar in North Queen Street. Some of my dad's brothers were also members of the team.

We lived at No. 17 Grove Street, a small, dimly lit street off

York Street. According to my mum, I was a nightmare for the first year as I was a 'real yappy baby'. I didn't need much sleep, but what I lost out in the cot I made up for in crying. I was so bad she said she felt like strangling me a few times. Even my aunts couldn't settle me, so it is no wonder my dad couldn't wait to get out to the pub for a bit of peace and quiet.

We wore hand-me-down clothes, and mine must have come from older children because they were always too big for me. We washed in a big tin bath and mum ran a metal comb through my hair to check for nits. If I fell, mum patched me up. I remember once having an infected finger; my dad took a red-hot needle and stuck it in my finger to break the skin; yellow poisonous puss oozed out. It was painful but it was effective. Thank God I never broke a leg; God knows what remedy my parents might have used!

Nobody could afford holidays; if you wanted to go to the seaside you were told to take a walk down to the docks. What you didn't have you didn't miss. We didn't have a dentist; a rotting tooth was removed by having a piece of string tied round it, with the other end tied to a door handle while my dad gave the door a sharp tug until the tooth came out. My parents would tell me not to worry, I would be okay. But nothing was further from the truth.

Our staple diet was porridge, potatoes and sausages, or an Ulster fry. Occasionally my mum would bake an apple pie. A Saturday night treat was pig's feet, tripe dripping in vinegar and home-made pea soup. That night the pubs would be packed with relatives and neighbours singing.

We were brought up never to steal, and the punishment came swift and hard. It was all right for your father to 'pick up' something from the docks, but kids could not steal. We never challenged the adult rules.

Our parents were sticklers for manners. We called the men 'Mister' and the women 'Mrs'. If you didn't learn manners they were beaten into you. We never answered back even if we thought we were right, but if we did we got a clip round the ear or the leg. Today this would be considered child cruelty, but my parents' old-fashioned ways taught me to respect my elders.

Outside our front door stood Gallaher's tobacco factory which provided much-needed jobs. The smell of tobacco filled the atmosphere. We also had several of Belfast's major linen mills on our doorstep, other great sources of employment.

We had very little crime at that time. The only transgressions were minor thefts from the docks to put food on the table. Everybody knew each other and relied on one another in times of need. Doors were left open and neighbours walked in and out. The only exception was the rent collector. We had an outside toilet and only cold running water. There was no such thing as carpets, just a thin sheet of lino. We were poor but we were a close-knit community.

We had our characters and many street fighters, like Buck Alec, who once worked for Al Capone. The Buck, as he was known, kept lions in the backyard of his Andrew Street home. The Buck's home was off-limits for any potential thief!

We stayed at Grove Street until I was over 2 years old. We moved then to Rathcoole which, though only six miles away, felt like moving to the countryside. It had 2,500 homes and was built by the then Housing Trust to relieve the pressure on a shortage of housing in Belfast. Our new house at Carnreagh Bend had three bedrooms, a kitchen and best of all an inside toilet and bathroom with hot water. It felt like my parents had won the pools and had bought a mansion. Although it was our new home, my parents still socialised in York Street as they found it hard to cut all ties with the area. My weekends too were spent with relatives in Grove Street playing football with my mates.

My sister Jean was quiet and never got into any trouble. She was the model sister and daughter, but my parents had no favourite and treated us as equals. To the people in Grove Street, Jean was like a little princess and I was the 'holy terror', which is why I knew the belt so well. Jean even went to elocution lessons which pleased my mum, my granny and my aunts. The only place I was sent to was my bedroom!

I was about 12 when I kicked a football and broke the window of a neighbour's house. My four friends and I ran away. By the time the police arrived I was in bed pretending to be asleep. Jean was looking after me when the policeman called. After he had gone I thought that was the end of the matter, but I got a rude awakening and was summoned downstairs by my dad. He took off his belt and he gave me what for around the legs.

Grove Street and Carnreagh Bend were light years apart. There was no grass in Grove Street. Our house there had a living room with a coal fire and a tiny scullery kitchen. A narrow, steep stairway took you up to two second floor bedrooms — one for my parents and one for Jean and me.

At the top of Grove Street was a small park with swings which was our 'amusement park' of the 1950s. Across the road was the mainly Catholic New Lodge district. Grove Street was one of five or six streets behind Gallaher's where many of our relatives lived. I felt part of a community where people were warm and friendly.

There were no televisions, but every house had a radio to hear the news. Other news came from the factory floor or the pub. On every street corner there was a pub in which most of the fathers played darts. Like old black and white movie scenes, these men in their cloth caps drank and played their games in a smoked-filled atmosphere. At closing time bare knuckle street fighters stood toe to toe in the street. Some fights lasted just a few seconds; others carried over to the next night. We were proud to say we came from York Street and we were the elite in Belfast. We disliked the Protestant people of the Shankill Road more than the Catholic community beside us.

Carnreagh Bend on the other hand was a modern home. As well as three bedrooms and an indoor bathroom, we had a cloakroom, a living room, a sitting room and gardens front and rear. It was so posh. Compared to the dark footpaths of Grove Street, Carnreagh Bend was lit up like a Christmas tree with working street lights.

However, I still looked forward to going back to Grove Street at the weekends to visit my relatives, particularly my Granny Elliott. She was my mother's mum and after my mum she was the kindest woman ever. She worked fourteen hours a day in the hotel kitchen at York Street Railway Station. Lizzie Elliott was built like Mike Tyson and no one dared cross her; she took no prisoners in an argument. But she was well known for her kindness and I always looked forward to visiting her in the hotel kitchen where I got ice cream and jelly, a real treat for a York Street child. Jean and I loved her very much and we still talk about her today. When I was around 11 or 12 Lizzie told me not to get into trouble and never bring the police to my mum's door. I followed her advice until my later years when the involvement of the police was unavoidable.

Lizzie had five children: Kathleen, my mum; Jimmy, a street fighter who was a kind and generous man but had the heart of a lion; Jean, my mum's younger sister; Andy, who was quiet and just enjoyed his beer; and Billy of whom she was very proud. Uncle Jimmy loved a good fist fight, even if he had to face several men on his own. He was the kind of character you never see any more. In his later years I would meet him in Belfast city centre and chat about the old days over a few pints. Sadly he died several years ago, but I will never forget him. He was hard on the outside but soft and kind inside. My Uncle Billy says I remind him of Jimmy with the fighting, which is a great compliment as Jimmy neither feared nor picked on anyone.

Although I was attached more to my mum's family, my father's siblings were also very kind and looked after everyone in the McCord family circle. York Street was full of McCords. While the mothers worked in the mills, the fathers generally earned a living from labouring or as tradesmen.

Young lads growing up in our area learned how to look after themselves; you had no other choice in those days. You never went crying to your mother that you had been hit. You had two choices: either get your older brother to do the fighting for you, or go and fight the boy again. It sounds rough, but that was the way it was then. Every family appeared to have a dad or an uncle who had a reputation for being a tough guy. None of my dad's brothers was classed as being a hard man, but they would band together when necessary.

My sister Jean went to the local primary school and always attended church. On Sunday mornings we went to church and in the afternoon to Sunday school. She became a born-again Christian and often talked to me about her faith, her relationship with the church and Jesus. But the church was not for me, and Jean and I agreed to disagree about religion. But she is loyal and would never hear a bad word said against me. I'm no angel and Jean accepts that. Her husband Eric and I get on great. As my mum puts it, 'Jean and Eric's marriage is a marriage made in heaven.' I'm sure over the years Jean often felt like sitting me down and giving me a good talking to, but in her heart she knew it would be a waste of time. I have lived my life rightly or wrongly and, as Jean would say, the Lord will be my judge.

My father Hector was a small, quiet man who would not hesitate to use his belt. He was always employed and I can't remember him missing work through sickness or hangovers. We never had a close bond that a father and son should have, even though I was his only son. When I compare our relationship to that which I have with my sons, I know how lucky a father I am. As he got older his hard centre softened and we grew closer. We often chatted over a pint of Guinness before he sadly died in 1994 aged 70.

My mum was the rock in our family and is the best mum, best granny and best great-granny. She has a heart of corn, always giving and taking nothing in return. I could never repay her in my lifetime for what she has done for me. She taught me to be brave, to stand up for myself and fight for what I believe in. 'Wee Kathleen' is an angel, my best friend and my mum. I have often given her an aching heart with my antics and for that I can't say sorry enough. She has the same traits as her mum: honesty, fearlessness and love. Whatever good there is in me is because of her. She had a hard life, working long hours in the mill to put a roof over our heads and food on the table. She often talked about her workmates which was a mixed workforce but which also had a strong bond. She still recalls working alongside Protestants from York Street and Catholics from the New Lodge area, in their bare feet just to earn a crust. Relatives and friends helped to look after the younger children so that the mums and dads could go to work.

Housing conditions were terrible but people still smiled.

Poverty knew no religious bounds and Catholic homes were the same as Protestant ones: cold, small and damp. Protestants voted for the Unionist parties, but in reality these politicians did nothing except keep the two communities divided by warning about the papist threat of a united Ireland and making them work for a pittance. There was a saying in Belfast that if you put a Union Jack on a monkey during the elections, the Protestants would vote for the monkey. How many monkeys were elected in the years gone by? Too many, but the people voted for them out of fear. My mum's generation now sees those politicians of yesteryear for what they were and how they played on their fears and took them for granted.

Life was always hard in working-class areas, where wages were so low. Religion was never mentioned in our street and the men drank in Catholic pubs in the area: the Gibraltar, the Brown Hen, Hannigan's, the Sportsman's, the Edinburgh Castle, the Terminus, the White Lion, the Cambridge, the Toddle Inn, Murphy's, and the Earl Inn. I was always in bed before my dad came home from the pub. After supper I was allowed outside for an hour and then straight to bed. The belt was a great timekeeper. Our front door was open from dusk till dawn with people popping in for a chat over a cup of tea. The streets were black with children playing who seemed much more content then than they do now. Despite the hardship the adults never moaned. This was York Street; this was Belfast and these were fiercely proud people.

I have the reputation of being a hard man, but in the 1950s you had real hard men who came home after street fights with the blood pouring from them for the women to clean them up. Today's so-called hard men of the paramilitary groups wouldn't have lasted a second in old York Street. In those days, it was bare knuckle fighting and then down to the pub afterwards. It was an education for a young man like me growing up in a hard man's world. You learned early on how to look after yourself.

One time my Uncle Jimmy and his mates got their hands on a large Christmas turkey. The only oven it would fit into was one at Granny Lizzie's hotel. She cooked it with lots of potatoes. Many houses enjoyed a first-rate Christmas dinner that year. The nearby docks allowed the men of York Street to earn extra money outside their wages. Selling contraband was a way of life and the proceeds were shared out among the people.

Sons followed in their fathers' footsteps. My granddad served in the army and fought in World War I. My Uncle Jimmy enlisted with the Royal Ulster Rifles, while my Uncle Andy joined the Merchant Navy. Jimmy was never out of trouble in the army and was more noted for fighting with his own than with the enemy! Despite this, no one had a bad word to say about him. When he died a few years ago of cancer, I heard stories about him which made me feel very proud of him. Even on his deathbed he never complained — a fighter, not a moaner. He had the heart of a lion and would have fought through a brick wall. He once told me: 'Don't let anyone walk on you.' He also told me to fight for what I believed in. I took heed of his advice and it worked most times, even if sometimes it was painful.

2.
Your Head's for Thinking, Your Fists for Fighting

The biggest day of my young life arrived when I started school at Whitehouse Primary which was a fifteen-minute walk from my Rathcoole home. Parents arrived early with their children in their neatly pressed uniforms and then left, looking back at the children and wondering how they would cope.

It was the first time any of us had been left with complete strangers, so it was heartbreaking to see our parents wandering off, not knowing if they would come back. I was one of the few who didn't cry. I just sat in silence staring at the strange children.

Some of the teachers put the fear of God into me and they could say or do what they wanted to you. I soon made friends, some I already knew from the streets but most I had never seen before. As well as a start in school education, it was also the start of the education of life — learning to look after yourself.

I always looked forward to the mid-morning break when we got the small 'dumpy' bottles of full cream milk. Lunchtime in the playground could be a nightmare where the quiet children would be picked on by the school bullies. But the bullies, for whatever reason, gave me a wide berth.

One of my teachers was known as Winnie the Witch. I was terrified of her. She gave you a withering look if your homework was not complete, followed by one of her tongue lashings. But her strict regime had the desired effect on me. Though she was strict, Winnie was probably one of the best teachers I ever had. Our teachers were so particular they even inspected our fingernails for dirt.

In my last two years at Whitehouse, my teacher was a former RAF member. A strict disciplinarian, he thrashed my hands many times with a cane. He had a son who got on well with everybody but fell victim to the bullies. His father didn't seem to care so I took him under my wing. As a reward, his father invited me to his house with his son, but the day ended in disaster when I opened the cages containing his fluffy pet hamsters and set them free in the back garden. The teacher was so angry. Strangely, he never invited me back! Weeks later, the devil inside me was at work again, this time catching a mouse and putting it in a girl's schoolbag. When she later opened her bag, the mouse jumped out and frightened the life out of her. I thought I would get away with it, but I was named to the hamster-lover who gave me a ferocious caning. I never felt pain like it, and the look on his face showed he was enjoying it. He got his revenge.

My favourite teacher was the headmaster Mr Lowry. He had an eleventh commandment which changed daily from either 'Thou shalt not give up' or 'Thou can do better.' He treated all the pupils the same, taught us respect and made sure we left school better mannered and better educated.

I passed the 11-plus and I decided to go to Belfast High School with a brand new uniform and cap. I had to take the bus the three or four miles from Rathcoole to Greenisland.

On my first day I realised I was no longer the tough guy from Whitehouse Primary. Bullying was rife and the older lads came looking for the new arrivals like lambs to the slaughter, 'ducking' their heads under the outside taps out of which ran icy cold water. It was sheer hell for first year pupils but it was part and parcel of their induction.

My new school introduced me to middle-class pupils for the first time. Snobbery had finally arrived in my life, and the snobs thought they were better than me, an ordinary working-class lad. Many of the teachers were also snobs who looked down their noses at us. On Friday afternoons the names were posted up on notice boards beside the lockers, of the pupils who had been reported by the prefects — more snobs in my eyes. And every Friday my name was on the notice board for the most minor of indiscretions. Punishment included detention, extra homework, lines or a visit to the headmaster for six of the best.

I remember one time one of the older pupils bullying a friend of mine. I stepped in and punched him on the side of the face, deflating his ego. Blue murder followed in the cloakroom and it took both myself and my friend to subdue the older fellow. On another occasion a middle-class pupil picked on me and started to pull at the leather patches on my blazer, calling me a tramp. They had been sewn on by my mum who said it would make my blazer last longer. I showed him no mercy and hit with my fists and feet. I was dispatched to the headmaster's office where the most cruel man I had ever met sat behind his desk. I received a thrashing with his favourite cane, but even though it was painful I refused to cry. The only teacher who came to my aid was my gym instructor who led me outside and put my hands under cold running water. He had a look of disgust for what my out-of-control headmaster had done to me.

Rugby was the main school sport, not soccer. I honestly enjoyed rugby as it was a legitimate way of fighting against posh schools like Methodist College (Methody), Instonians (Inst), Campbell College, and Belfast Royal Academy (BRA), our greatest rival both on and off the pitch. One time our coach told me to make sure a BRA player knew he was going to be involved in a hard game, so I hit him a couple of punches in the face, forcing him to leave the pitch. The next morning at assembly the headmaster announced that I had to report to his office. He snapped at me, saying the school had received a complaint of assault from BRA. But instead of the cane, this time I got a few hours' detention, probably because we had won the game. My thirst for sport soon caught the eye of the coaches who selected me for the senior team. It was a big step up and I often got thumped or punched. My face often looked like a butcher's apron.

I had a few girlfriends, but at the age of 15 my heart started to throb like never before for the most beautiful girl I had ever seen who lived in Rathcoole but didn't go to my school. Vivienne was her name and she had stolen my heart. We would later marry and Vivienne bore me three of the most beautiful sons a father could ever wish for.

Because we were so young, older people told us not to get too involved. But that wasn't for me. Raymond McCord, the young man who loved football, rugby and fighting, had fallen in love with a beautiful girl at 15. I was totally smitten by her looks, her kindness and generosity, and defended her against all-comers. It is true that you never forget your first love, but sometimes you don't appreciate what you have, and that includes me. The one good thing that came out of it is that my sons will not be as stupid as me. Vivienne must have been sick to her back teeth of the fights I became embroiled in because I never walked away from one. Some of the scraps didn't even involve either myself or Vivienne. I would fight for those who couldn't stand up for themselves.

One night a relative rang me while I was working as a doorman to say three men were trying to kick in his door and his pregnant wife was terrified. I told him that I would call by when I finished work and if they returned to ring me immediately. When I had the club cleared around midnight, I called by his home to find his pregnant wife crying. They told me that the gang leader actually lived next door to them. I called at their next door neighbour's where a party was in full swing. A man opened the front door and I made it very plain that if he or his mates went to my relative's house again I would personally 'do' him. He told me to fuck off, so I punched him in the face and knocked him out. Revellers in the living room came out to see what the commotion was about. I sensed there could be more problems. Then I heard my relative's voice from behind me and over my shoulder saying, 'What are you doing, Raymond?' He looked down at his neighbour lying unconscious and said: 'You're at the wrong door, Raymond. It's the neighbour on the other side you're looking for.' Mistakes can happen. I told the party goers that somewhere, sometime, he had done something to deserve what he got. Some of his friends laughed; others didn't. To be honest, I never liked the man anyway because he was a member of a loyalist paramilitary group. He has never spoken to me since, but I haven't lost any sleep over him. I afterwards went to the right house and punched the guy who was sitting in his bedroom.

Another time I was working as a bouncer in a bar when a lad came out of the toilet bleeding and crying. Three men came out after him and the lad told me they had hit him for no reason. As I sat the terrified young lad down, two of the three loyalists came at me. I hit the first with a sweet left hook and he crumpled to the floor. The second felt my right fist thunder into his jaw. The third thug, a member of the Ulster Volunteer Force (UVF), ran out the back door and escaped. I grabbed his two friends one at a time and dumped them outside to sleep off their aching heads. That same night around 8.30, the one who got away appeared back at the bar with a few mates as back-up. I caught him with a right hand, and several of his teeth embedded in my fist. I ended up in the accident and emergency unit of Whiteabbey Hospital as my hand had swollen up like a balloon. I needed a tetanus injection, but as I have a fear of needles I could feel the colour drain from my face as the nurse dabbed my hip with a cotton swab before the needle was inserted. A nurse had found my Achilles' heel! The following Saturday, the man missing a few teeth appeared back at the bar with a pal. I hit him a thump on his jawbone and I told his accomplice that the reason why I hit him again was because I didn't like injections. He hadn't a clue what I was talking about, but I did.

I enjoyed working as a doorman. Some of the bouncers were great characters. In one bar I was put in charge of the doormen and had to sack a few for their attitude towards the customers. One of those I sacked was a UVF man from Monkstown and a police informant. Another doorman was Big Frank who was as tough as old boots, a good friend and a top bouncer. Then there was my cousin Robert who was as strong as an ox and feared no one. We were in many fights together, had a strong blood bond and we both hated the paramilitaries. I haven't seen Robert for over ten years and sadly he died towards the end of last year. His health hadn't been great. Early last year he was attacked in his house by the UVF, who burned him on several parts of his body. Ten years earlier they wouldn't have darkened his door.

My only explanation for fighting is that I wanted to stand

up for those less fortunate than myself. I was a regular visitor to the hospitals, with broken hands, broken legs, a busted nose once or twice, split lips and a few black eyes. The wounds of battle earned you respect in Rathcoole. But now I say to any young man: walk away when you can. It sounds rich coming from me, but I know I could have been seriously injured if not killed many times. I must have been blessed with good luck. I still fight but now it's about survival, not about being a tough guy. Anyway, most fights just aren't worth it.

I was in a club one night in the Rathcoole area with a couple of mates having a drink when this big guy came up and stood beside us to have his drink. He started to get nasty to one of my friends. To avoid trouble we hit the dance floor, but he followed us. When we returned to the bar, there he was at our side and started on us again. One of my friends offered to fight him outside. As soon as the big guy said yes, my friend threw a punch but missed. The man grabbed my mate's hand and laughed in his face. A waitress told him to behave himself and he turned on her. I can't stand men cursing at women, so I told him to shut up and move off. Arrogantly he then told me that he was going to bust me. Vivienne, who was by then my wife and who was sitting with one of her sisters, got up when she heard him threaten me. She tried to talk sense into him, whereupon he then became nasty towards her. Could he not see she was trying to do him a favour? I offered him a fight outside. As we got to the door he tried to punch me when I wasn't looking, but I caught on and I punched him to the floor. Five minutes later he came back in and told me I was going to get a digging. He obviously hadn't learned his lesson and when I punched him on the jaw, this time he stayed down. He later said I got lucky twice that night.

The staff contacted his wife who came and collected him. I went home thinking it was all over, but the next day when I returned to the club and had just sat down, an old man started to lecture me about fighting. Just then I was told by a staff member that the police were outside looking for me. I went out and the uniformed RUC officers told me I had to go with them to the police station to be questioned about an alleged assault the previous night. Before I could answer, an off-duty detective who had been sitting near us the night before, arrived for a drink. He had a chat with his uniformed colleagues and after ten minutes he came back into the bar and told me everything would be all right. He explained to the police that I was only defending myself.

The old man who had been giving me the lecture was stopped in his tracks by what the off-duty detective had to say. The big guy I had knocked out twice was another off-duty policeman. I was still taking in this news when the old man stood up, shook my hand, bought me a pint and a small whisky and told me I was perfectly right. He hated most policemen and from that day on I was his best mate. He went home that night with his pockets a little lighter.

Once on 12 July, the day when Orangemen parade across Northern Ireland, I was going into a pub for a quiet drink. The owner, a friend of mine, and his son were being beaten by two men. I stepped in and hit the one attacking his son and then pulled the bigger man off the pub owner. He threw a punch at me, missed, and I hit him so hard he fell to the ground. Afterwards I went into the pub with the owner for a bottle of Guinness. That night, as I was working on the door at the pub, I got a pleasant surprise when an American friend of the owner I had helped came up to me, shook my hand and said it was the first real street fight he had seen in years, and thanked me. When I shook his hand I felt something in his grip. It was a gold watch, his way of thanking me for helping his friend. It was the first reward I had ever received for fighting. Unfortunately I lost the watch some years later. David McKittrick, a respected journalist and author, once wrote an article on me in the *Belfast Telegraph*, saying I was Belfast's champion bare knuckle fighter. It was a nice compliment but totally wrong. All I am is a father who will fight anyone who goes against my family with threats and intimidation. The difference between me and the paramilitaries is that I would die for my cause, my family.

3.
Paramilitaries were Not for Me

Rathcoole was under the control of two loyalist paramilitary groups, the Ulster Defence Association (UDA) and the Ulster Volunteer Force (UVF), the older of the two organisations. Men who had grown up with me in Rathcoole or had gone to school with me had overnight become the great 'protectors' of the people, but their only interest was lining their own pockets.

My early years in Rathcoole went so fast. It was no time from when we moved from York Street to Rathcoole until I was getting married and raising three children. Few would believe it, but Protestants and Catholics lived together and religion was the last thing on our minds, surfacing only around 12 July each year. Protestant and Catholic kids played football together in the streets. It became so popular we formed street teams, arranging weekly matches. It was like we had formed our very own Premiership. We had no referees so the occasional fight broke out, but it was never anything too serious.

Until the advent of the Troubles people lived happily side by side and socialised together at the weekends. One of our neighbours had a phone in their house which seemed like the ultimate luxury item. But the real deal then was a garden and suddenly there was an army of green fingers in Rathcoole. The Housing Trust sent out rent collectors every week who apart from collecting the rent also carried out inspections of front gardens, telling people to cut their grass or pull out unsightly weeds. The garden 'police' had arrived.

When the Troubles began in 1969, the tranquillity of Rathcoole was shattered. Rioting erupted in Belfast and Derry. People were being shot dead and in some parts of Belfast whole streets were burned to the ground. Protestant vigilantes patrolled our estate which had now lost its cross-community make-up. As a 15-year old I found it hard to understand how people could hate each other for their religion. In my street my Catholic friends were intimidated. Protestant teenagers formed a gang called the KAI. I gave it a wide berth and I continued to have both Catholic and Protestant friends. At the dead of night the windows of Catholic homes were smashed. Soon the UDA emerged and the young Protestant men of Rathcoole flocked to join. Rathcoole was now an estate of 'tough guys' whose targets were Catholic families. My father and I argued many times over these issues as he became involved in the UDA.

My first brush with the UDA came when I was 16. I was lying in bed one night around 11 o'clock and I could hear someone lifting the milk bottles from our doorstep. I opened the front door to find a crowd standing at the bottom of our pathway holding the stolen milk bottles. I asked them what they were doing. The mob, who were wearing scarves or handkerchiefs to disguise their faces, told me to go back into the house and close the door. I did the opposite and went down the pathway to confront them. One of the gang looked over his shoulder towards the home where my Catholic friend Jimmy and his family lived and motioned that they were going to attack it. I told them Jimmy was my best mate. Then my dad appeared and asked what was going on. A few of the thugs called him over and my dad was able to temporarily calm the situation and stop the thugs from attacking Jimmy's home. However, from around the corner I heard someone yell out. The younger UDA element were attacking Jimmy and trying to break his arm. My father and I stopped them and rescued Jimmy, taking him back to our house. We rang for an ambulance and Jimmy was treated for just minor injuries in hospital. As a result of this attack his parents decided to move out for the safety of their family. Their home was snapped up by a Protestant family who had been intimidated out of their Belfast home, so the UDA's plan of turning Rathcoole into a loyalist Catholic-free ghetto was taking root. Some people were like sheep and wanted to follow; that wasn't going to happen to me.

When the RUC could not hold the line, the British government airlifted in soldiers from mainland Britain and soon troops were patrolling Rathcoole. Life had changed for the worse. With soldiers on the streets, UDA men called to talk to my father who by this time was a senior UDA member. I resented these men calling at our home and at times I made it clear to them what I thought of them and their behaviour. The soldiers couldn't stop the rise in sectarianism. One young 16-year-old Catholic who was sitting with his Protestant girlfriend was shot by the UDA several times. Thankfully he survived, but his family left Northern Ireland for good after that. It made me ashamed to be a Protestant. As the violence increased, more and more young men, some of them my friends, were swelling the UDA ranks. I wasn't the only young man who refused to join; other friends like Louis, John, Jimmy, Robert and Angus didn't fall for the UDA lies.

The Troubles intensified during 1970 and murder became more and more frequent. One Catholic victim, Liam McDonald, 16, who lived at the bottom of my street, was shot dead. The UVF had also started to kill Catholics, yet not one of their victims was an IRA member. Eventually, with few Catholics left in Rathcoole to shoot, loyalist terrorists turned their guns on their own community, killing people or carrying out punishment shootings.

Despite the violence, Vivienne and I continued our relationship and in 1973, aged 20, we got married and set up home in a flat in Rathcoole. I remember one night sitting in the flat with Vivienne and hearing the sound of breaking glass and screaming. The homes of Catholic families were being targeted by paramilitaries. As morning broke, a cavalcade of removal lorries left the estate with the families' rescued belongings. During the intimidation, a busload of young men from Rathcoole were caught by the police after they attacked a public house and several men inside were shot dead. All the men in the bus went to jail, some of them friends of mine. They regretted getting on the bus. One of them told me he thought he was going for a day's drinking.

My early experiences in Rathcoole helped to shape me for my adult life. I had long-running battles with both the UDA and the UVF and I had to fight members of both organisations because I was not going to be bullied. In February 1992 I went to my local pub, the Fern Lodge, for a couple of pints with some friends. Standing near us was a UDA crowd who supported John 'Grug' Gregg who was later to become the organisation's south east Antrim brigadier. They kept their eyes on me and I asked them were they looking for me. Six weeks earlier, two UDA men had tried to shoot me but their guns jammed. Their excuse for trying to kill me was that I had been bad-mouthing Gregg, which I hadn't. An RUC Land Rover was parked outside the home of one of the gunmen all night as they must have been expecting something to happen. We will never know, and only the police can answer for their actions that night.

When I approached the UDA group and asked them about it myself, they said the matter was now closed and they didn't want any trouble with me. As the night went on, more and more UDA men swelled the bar and the Fern Lodge manager advised me to leave by the back door. I stood my ground and later went to the toilet, only to be followed by a few UDA men. A few words were spoken between us, but I left without a mark. However, the UDA men who 'slipped in the toilets' had one or two problems! As I walked back into the bar I could see a UDA lynch mob outside the front door. The fun wasn't too far away, I thought. A friend also advised me to slip out the side door where another friend was waiting in his car to get me away safely. But it wasn't in my nature to run. I came in by the front door and I would leave by the same route.

I took off my coat and walked out the front door, believing one of my friends was with me. I was wrong; he had disappeared. He later claimed the UDA held him at gunpoint in the toilets, but he had lied to me. Outside all hell broke loose and the baying UDA mob hit me with whatever they had in their hands. I never stood a chance. I was left unconscious outside the pub. But the mob hadn't finished. As I lay motionless on the ground they dropped heavy paving stones on my legs and arms and also smashed up my face, leaving me for dead. They stopped a waitress from making an emergency call, but fortunately a passing RUC patrol came to my aid. One officer held me up to stop me choking on my own blood. I woke up for a moment or two and then I passed out in his arms.

The next thing I remember is waking up in hospital fighting for my life. My family were sent for as my injuries were so severe. I looked like Elephant Man, my face all swollen. My father almost fainted when he first saw me and the doctors told my mother that it was my heart that had kept me alive. At the request of the RUC, the medical staff moved me into a secure private room and I was given round-the-clock armed police protection as I had named some of my attackers to the detectives. The UDA sent a man to my hospital bed, asking me to keep quiet and not talk to the police. This was the same low-life scumbag who had hidden in the toilets on the night of the assault. I gave him a sharp reply: 'Clear off and tell your UDA friends I will be naming them to the police.' I was not going to be told what not to do. During my hospital stay the UDA repeatedly tried to get in touch with me, once even sending a top Shankill Road loyalist to see me, but I told him also to get lost. I remained in hospital for some weeks with two broken legs pieced back together using screws and pins.

After recovering, I took the bus to Rathcoole and, on crutches and with my face stitched up, hobbled to the door of the UDA's south east Antrim brigadier and called on him to come out and face me. But he didn't come out; instead he phoned the police. When they arrived, the officers couldn't believe their eyes. Although they arrested me, I was later released without charge.

The UDA were desperate to keep the men who had assaulted me out of jail. They offered me a deal: retract my statement to the RUC and I would not be harmed. At a meeting held in east Belfast, I was told in no uncertain terms that if I went to court and gave evidence against the five men who had been charged, I would be shot dead. When the deal was offered, I countered with another: if the five men charged with assaulting me would fight me one at a time, then I would agree to the deal. My attitude was that it was better to settle the dispute in the street than in court. But all five declined my generous offer, including the brigadier's second-in-command. In the end the UDA deal was now off the table and during the three years it took for their case to come to trial, I had little trouble from the UDA. It seemed the organisation had learned a lesson: I would not be bullied. Strangely, during the wait for the trial, someone was attacking UDA men and their homes. No one ever discovered who was doing it, but it worried the hell out of the UDA leaders in Rathcoole.

The day finally came in 1995 for the start of the trial at the Crumlin Road Courthouse in north Belfast. The UDA flooded the courthouse with their own men in an attempt to intimidate me into withdrawing my evidence. Convicted UDA double killer John White asked me not to give evidence, but I told him where to go. The non-jury Diplock trial lasted five days but it was a farce. Up until this time I had believed in the British justice system, but this trial destroyed my faith in it. Five guilty men in my eyes walked free from the court and I knew the UDA would come after me. They had shot up the homes of two of my family and attacked one of my sons, the biggest mistake they could make. The three paramilitary thugs who had beaten up my eldest son Raymond were mysteriously beaten up by an individual with no baseball bat or weapons. When one of them picked on Raymond again, he received another visit from an individual who liked to operate on his own. However this thug refused to learn from his mistakes and after hitting another son, Gareth, he received a further visit to his home. In full view of his neighbours, the thug was given a severe beating. As the story goes, he was warned that every time his attacker saw him, he would chin him. This individual kept his word and the thug eventually left for England for a peaceful life.

Following the court case, the UDA smashed up my car. Quite suddenly UDA cars were being smashed and burned outside their homes. The new brigadier, John 'Grug' Gregg, stepped up UDA intimidation of my family, and shots were fired into the homes of my family. I was told the gunmen hadn't even bothered to wear masks during the attacks. My son Gareth actually chased the gunmen with a poker in his hand.

On one occasion I brought Gareth to the house of a UDA bouncer who had attacked him as part of a punishment squad. I told Gareth to sit in the car and watch. I went to the man's door and called him out. As the thug stood in front of me I told him I was going to let him punch me the way he had hit Gareth. He thought this was his lucky night. But as he was about to throw his punch I knocked him out with a right hand. I looked at him and said, 'I lied.' The smile on Gareth's face made it all worthwhile.

On another occasion I was visiting my son Raymond, who was in the Royal Air Force, when I missed my flight home. I was to be home in time to take my mother to my sister's house in Rathcoole. I rang my sister about the delay, only to be told that her house, and Vivienne's home too, had been shot up the previous night. I rang the RUC and asked what they were doing about it. All they could say was they were making enquiries. When I told them that I would find out myself who carried out the shootings, the police said that if I did anything then I would be arrested. When I got back home, I immediately checked on my family and was relieved everyone was all right. The police were given the names and addresses of those who had carried out the shootings and who had ordered it. However, no one was arrested and it has since become clear to me that those involved were police informants. But before I could get to speak to some of these individuals about the attacks on the McCord family homes, someone took it upon himself to shoot up UDA homes. I was arrested a few times and on one occasion I was held in Castlereagh Interrogation Centre in Belfast for three days over one of the shootings but was released without charge. I was an innocent man, yet the UDA gangsters who shot up my family's homes were never arrested.

Fate has sometimes a strange way of working and some years later those who had become involved in the attacks on my family became *personae non gratae* with the UDA leadership. At last the bully boys were receiving a hefty dose of their own medicine. Three of those who were either directly or indirectly involved in trying to kill me died violent deaths — two were shot dead and a third died in an accident. This was a personal vendetta by one UDA brigade as opposed to the whole UDA organisation turning against me. I remember meeting UDA members from other brigades who told me they were disgusted at my treatment. These things happened because I beat Grug in a fair fight.

Sometimes I wish I had taken my family from Northern Ireland. I did try once to emigrate to Australia, but I was turned down. Life could have been so much different for us all. But facing down paramilitaries means there can only be one outcome — trouble. People have wondered why I never joined the loyalist paramilitaries. It would have been easier to say yes to these organisations, but thank God I have always taken the hard way in life.

4.
Sandsy, Me and Star of the Sea

Bobby Sands is renowned throughout the world as an IRA hunger striker who starved himself to death for his republican beliefs on 5 May 1981. He died in the Maze Prison after sixty-six days on a fast-to-death protest over the wearing of prison issue clothing.

The Bobby Sands who became a household name more than twenty-six years ago was not the Sandsy I had known growing up in Rathcoole. I never thought he would have become a leading republican and IRA man. Unfortunately he was like many young men who fell into the hands of paramilitaries.

I was once asked what I thought of Sandsy and I replied that he was like me and the rest of our team — football mad. We played for the under-16 Star of the Sea team. We had a great team spirit and there was no politics or sectarianism. We just talked and played football.

Even though Star of the Sea youth club was looked upon as being Catholic, it was run by a Doctor Conlon who didn't tolerate sectarianism. He was a fair man and treated everyone equally, irrespective of their religion. The only reason I was playing for the Star was because there was no junior team in Rathcoole that played in any local league or competition.

With a blend of Protestants and Catholics, the under-16 team became the most successful side in junior football, but we were never looked upon as a mixed religion team. We were fit and happy 15 and 16-year olds who loved the thrill of competition and we feared no one.

We played in the Down and Connor League which was made up of Catholic teams, the Northern Ireland Boys League and also Protestant sides. The Star had six Protestant members, some of whom later joined loyalist paramilitary groups. Two Protestant members of our team, Terry Nicholl and Michael Acheson, joined the UVF and were later convicted of terrorist offences. Terry was one of my best friends and he went to Belfast High School with me. He was a talented player, hard in the tackle but also very skilful on the ball. Michael relied heavily on his defensive abilities and took no prisoners during matches. He was our Chopper Harris.

Then there was Sandsy who was already in the Maze Prison serving a fourteen year sentence for possessing a revolver when Terry and Michael were jailed. He later became an IRA leader in the Maze and subsequently MP for Fermanagh/South Tyrone. Sandsy was like Forrest Gump and could run all day. He wasn't the most skilful of players, but he always gave 100 per cent every game.

The other members of our team were: Dessie Black (Catholic); Geordie Hussey (Protestant); Willie Caldwell (P); Tommy O'Neill, Sandsy's best mate (C); Denis Sweeney who is now a doctor (C); John Corbett (P); Paddy Davidson who had a brother murdered by loyalist paramilitaries (C); and Brendan Nellis, the Nobby Stiles in our team (C). Three of the team — myself, Denis Sweeney and Tommy O'Neill —

played for the Northern Ireland Boys Club international team. I was fortunate enough to play for them for three years in a row and for the last two years I was made team captain. It was a fantastic time playing for my country with Tommy and Denis in the same team.

That Star team was the best at the time, fondly remembered and revered in footballing circles. Though the Troubles were just starting in 1969, the team remained conflict free and Dr Conlan made sure of that. Even though I was the last Protestant player at the club, I never once contemplated leaving. It was like a big family with the Doc as the head. I'm convinced the U-16 team was the Doc's best because of our success.

By day he was the doctor at aircraft makers Short Brothers and Harland in east Belfast where he used his position to secure work for many young men in the club. He did the same with his position on the board of the Northern Ireland Police Authority. With influence in high places, he helped to keep many young men on the straight and narrow.

The Doc was strict and it was for this reason that the youth club was so successful. He kept the club going with his own money and was the club's engine room. Nobody ever forgot him and when he died in 1994, the chapel was packed with past and present members and ordinary Protestant people who came to pay their respects. His legacy was the cross-community team he had built and I believe he wanted people to live the same way, Catholics and Protestants living peacefully side by side. When the Troubles started, most of the Protestants left the club. However, I decided to continue playing for the Star despite the many arguments I had with friends and family. My father and his UDA friends were none too pleased that I was still playing for the club, but it was my decision.

In 1969 we reached the final of the Down and Connor League which was played at Celtic Park in west Belfast. There was a good crowd in because after the final there was to be greyhound racing on the track that ran round the outside of the pitch. Our opponents were St Paul's from west Belfast, our main rivals in the league. There was no love lost between us and the game quickly turned into a needle match. Every ball was keenly contested. It wasn't a match for the faint hearted.

I played at centre-half and scored the equaliser after St Paul's took the lead. After my goal, the tackling became much more ferocious, to the delight of the crowd. In the end we ran out 5-1 winners which sparked a massive free-for-all on the pitch. I can still see Sandsy with a football boot in his hand hitting one of the St Paul's players over the head with it! With the cup and our medals, we headed off to a chippie for fish and chips washed down with a bottle of Coke each.

We went on to win more leagues and trophies, but success was not always measured on the pitch; it was also gauged on how well you could use your fists. One time we were playing in the nationalist Ardoyne area in north Belfast and had just beaten the local youth team when punches were thrown just before the final whistle. After getting changed, the opposition were waiting for us and pelted us with stones and bottles. We took to our heels as the missiles rained down on us, but we got our revenge at the return match with another win.

We were fit and healthy young men with a glad eye for the ladies and we would go on the pull at the Friday night disco in St Patrick's School known as Barney's on Belfast's Antrim Road. The local Catholic gangs, many of whom played in our league, were at the disco looking for trouble. One Friday I was sitting at a table talking to a few girls when I noticed my friends had got into trouble with the bouncers. One of my friends shouted for me to come and help him, but by the time I got to him, four or five of our gang were lying bleeding on the floor. I was on my own. When the bouncers asked me if I was with them, I replied no and was allowed to stay in the club.

A girl then came over to me and said that a Catholic gang from the New Lodge Road had arrived and knew I was at the disco. I could see them moving from table to table looking for me. My saviour came in the form of Gerry 'Yogi' McKenna, one of my Catholic friends from the New Lodge Road, who was an amateur boxer and a tough guy. The gang of Catholic lads came over to my table and told Yogi they were going to 'do' me, give me a good kicking. Yogi laid down the ground rules — I would take them on one at a time. The gang had a different view. Yogi and I decided to go outside with the gang and sort things out. Near the exit I thought about asking the bouncers to help, but Yogi whispered some advice in my ear. As I stepped outside I took off like the wind up the Antrim Road while Yogi held the door shut long enough for me to escape.

At the rematch the following week we evened up the odds when I turned up with Sandsy, Tommy O'Neill, Terry Nicholl and a few others. The Catholic gang never counted on me returning, never mind returning with members of the Star team. We looked after each other on and off the pitch.

Sandsy loved running, particularly road running, and once the club sent five or six of us to Newry in Co. Down to take part in a road race. The first in our team was Paddy Davidson who was an ace runner. That night we were all sitting inside the Bosco club whose most famous player was goalkeeper Pat Jennings, who later played for Arsenal, Tottenham and Northern Ireland. The race had been delayed and a row broke out between some of our team. Sandsy and

I were arguing after he took sides with his mate Tommy O'Neill and the row ended with me punching Sandsy in the face. On our return journey to Rathcoole the fight wasn't even mentioned.

We would go out on dates together with our girlfriends. I had my Vivienne; Sandsy and Tommy were also going out with girls. On a Sunday night we would go down to the club disco. I loved bringing Vivienne to the club as she was the best looking girl in Rathcoole. Sandsy was doing a line with a girl called Geraldine who lived ten doors from me. They later got married. When the Troubles started they left and I only ever saw Geraldine once after that. Sandsy was in jail near the end of his sentence when I bumped into her. I asked her how Sandsy was doing and she told me he would be out of jail soon. I told her to tell him I was asking about him. Geraldine and I spoke for a while and then we parted. The only time I saw her again was on television after Sandsy died. I have often wondered how she felt about Sandsy going on hunger strike and did she ever try to talk him out of it. The Geraldine that I knew was a nice quiet girl whereas Sandsy was the opposite. The face staring out of republican murals is not the Sandsy I knew. He was a young man led by the Troubles and older men into the IRA.

During a television programme made about him after he died, some of the U-16 team were interviewed. Geordie Hussey, another good Star player, said he left the team as a result of the Troubles but never criticised the players or the club. When I was asked about Sandsy, I said he was a good, hard left back. I said I only knew Sandsy the footballer, not Bobby Sands the IRA man. Denis Sweeney told the programme he didn't like Sandsy. He also spoke of our football team and what it was like playing with Protestants. It was amazing to hear him say that we were the first

Protestants he really knew and played football with as he lived in a Catholic area.

Terry Nicholl was a gifted footballer who had the talent to play in the Irish League. We were the same age and lived together in Rathcoole, but I only got to know him when we started going to High School. He was a tough lad and we didn't hit it off at the start. When the Troubles broke out, he left the Star team saying he had a choice to make. Terry chose the UVF, but I didn't know he had joined until he was arrested for attempted armed robbery. During his time in jail I went to visit him in Magilligan Prison and he didn't seem to have a worry in the world. That was just Terry, but he paid a price and lost his loving girlfriend. Terry is still a good friend who never ignored me or tried to avoid me over my problems with the UVF. He was brought up as a Mormon, not as a Protestant, and later visited his sister in Salt Lake City. However, US Immigration refused to allow him to stay and start a new life there because of his criminal record. We still meet for a few beers and talk about the old days.

At the age of 17 I had trials with Blackpool FC and Manchester United. I lived in Manchester for six weeks while I was training with United, but I came home because Vivienne was on her own in Rathcoole. I have never regretted that decision as I was in love. The heart ruled the head. Terry Nicholl, Tommy O'Neill and Denis Sweeney also had trials in England. Denis eventually swapped his boots for a stethoscope, but he had it all in his locker. Hard in the tackle, lightning fast and skilful on the ball, if he hadn't gone to university who knows how far he would have gone in football. Denis was one of the Northern Ireland Boys Club international team and he and my friend Yogi McKenna and I played a game against England at Bedford City's ground, drawing the match 1-1. Afterwards we were invited to a reception and as team captain I was asked to make a speech. Halfway through, the police came in and informed the Northern Ireland officials that my father was in hospital in Bedford. He had decided to fly over to England to watch me but got mugged while asking for directions. Yogi went with me to the hospital. My father discharged himself despite his injuries. We went to the nearest police station where my father made a statement. We then went out in a police minibus looking for the muggers. When my father spotted three of the lads who had assaulted him, the police gave us a choice — deal with them ourselves or take them to court. We decided to mete out our own form of justice.

Michael Acheson was another player in our team who went to jail. A talented defender, Michael didn't live too far away from the club. He was a Protestant and after leaving the Star he too joined the UVF, which surprised me as he was only ever interested in football and girls. However, Michael foolishly became involved in the bombing of a Catholic pub in Greencastle in north Belfast and was jailed for eighteen years. After leaving prison, Michael turned his back on the paramilitaries, starting a new life and a new family.

Big Paddy Davidson, another true Star friend, had a brother murdered during the Troubles, but it was never spoken about at our club. Dessie Black, a Catholic and our goalkeeper, and Willie Caldwell, a Protestant, both moved to Guernsey in the Channel Islands. Dessie became manager of a ladies' football team and I have not seen him since. Willie has returned home a few times and we met up to discuss old times over a beer. Brendy 'Nobby Stiles' Nellis was one of the hardest tacklers I have ever seen. Many a player hobbled away from him nursing a sore leg. He was a true gentleman and became involved in youth work, keeping kids away from crime and the paramilitaries. In the older Star team was gentleman Marty Quinn, a good friend and the current manager at Coleraine FC. Others in the senior squad were Jimmy Doherty, Brian Shortt, Tommy Walsh, John 'Butch' Crangle and Tommy Wilson. They were all older than me, but I was happy playing alongside them. The senior team, aged 21–40, played in the Amateur League and we had problems with some Protestant teams. I was still only 16 or 17 when we played a match against an all-Protestant team. Micky McGinn tackled one of the opposition and the two of them fell to the ground. As Micky was getting to his feet, a big guy from the other team head butted him. I was nearest to the incident and I ran over and kicked him where it hurt. As he lay on the ground, he looked up at me and said: 'He's a Prod too!' The referee, who was the opposing team's manager, sent him off for the head butting incident but let me off with a warning.

It soon became too dangerous for me to play for the Star because of the sectarian murders and I would have been a sitting duck leaving the Star club at night. Today the Star is more famous for basketball, which I find very sad. I have gone to the club a few times, looked around and the memories come flooding back. They feel so real I can almost touch them. I have often wondered how far that team would have gone if they hadn't broken up.

The Star wasn't lucky because I played for them. I was lucky, honoured and privileged to play for Star of the Sea. Maybe one day there will be another Star of the Sea to match our 1960s squad.

5.
The Shipyard and the Foundry

If I wasn't going to earn a living at football, then I had to put my hands to use and get a job as a tradesman. Football and Manchester United were my passion and Georgie Best was my hero, but none of these was going to put a roof over my head.

Harland and Wolff shipyard (the Yard) was the biggest employer which had the largest dry dock in the world. It had built many famous ships including the *Titanic*, its sister ship RMS *Olympic* as well as HMS *Britannia* and the SS *Canberra*.

The Yard had a predominantly Protestant workforce and sons followed in their fathers' footsteps as apprentice welders, joiners or blacksmiths. Many men lost their lives at the Yard as the safety then was nothing like today. There was no such thing as hard hats and working high above ground was extremely dangerous. But there was a real camaraderie among the workers and the laughter kept the men going through the hard times as there were frequent rounds of redundancies as orders dropped off.

When the Troubles started, the Yard became a hotbed of loyalist paramilitaries where Catholics became easy targets for intimidation and murder. Catholic welder Maurice O'Kane, whom I knew quite well, was shot dead by the UVF while working on a vessel. He was a decent man doing an honest day's work. Intimidation was rife but people just turned a blind eye to it.

It may have been dangerous but I worked alongside some interesting characters with nicknames like the Screaming Skull, the Spitting Pig, Geordie Sore Toes, Blondie, Rocket Man and one called Seldom who did little work. We laughed and joked over a strong cup of tea which was brewed in large, old food tins. The water was boiled over an oxy-acetylene cutting torch. We didn't have teabags, just big spoonfuls of loose tea tossed into the can. The stuff was so black it was like drinking tar. Like everything in life, you got used to it because that's all we had to wash down our thick sliced 'pieces'.

Many stories emanated from the docks. A steelworker who had worked all his life there, one day after work committed suicide and left a note with instructions for his body to be cremated and his ashes scattered into the sea water at the yard. His wishes were carried out to the letter.

As the years passed, safety got more priority and accidents became fewer. But noise was a constant problem and many workers suffered from ruptured ear drums. Their union lodged claims for industrial deafness. One steelworker who I will call 'Sam' from east Belfast appeared in court as a test case for the claims. The judge asked him if he had ever played in a band. Sam asked him to speak up.

In a louder voice the judge said: 'Did you ever play in a band?'

'No, never,' replied Sam.

'Did you ever work in a noisy environment?'

Sam just stared at the judge and said: 'Could you speak up, your honour.'

The judge was beginning to lose his temper and barked at Sam: 'Did you ever work in a noisy environment?'

With a straight face Sam replied: 'No, your honour. I never worked on a Saturday or a Sunday in my life!'

Sam, whose hearing was normally pin sharp, won several thousand pounds in compensation.

I couldn't afford a car, so I depended on getting a lift to and from work. My foreman then was Big Frank, six foot tall and a real big softie at heart. And for a 'sloper' like me, someone who knocked off early before quitting time, I couldn't have asked for a better foreman. Each day a couple of 'stagers', men who put up the scaffolding planks, would give me the nod when they were ready for home. One morning Big Frank told me about an incident at his house the night before when a gunman tried to rob him. I told him I would speak to a few people to make sure he wouldn't have to go through a similar ordeal. Later that day the two stagers signalled to me that they were going home. The next morning Big Frank told the two stagers and me that we shouldn't have done what we did. Apparently three men abducted a man where Big Frank lived and shot him in the legs. Nothing would convince him that we had nothing to do with it. The upside was that for months I was home early every day.

One of the Yard's most colourful characters was the late Frank 'Pootsy' Millar, or as his opponents called him, 'Super Prod'. He knew my family from York Street and had a reputation as a street fighter and as a bigot. Though I never heard him say anything anti-Catholic, I nevertheless believe he was. Millar was an Independent Unionist councillor and was one of Belfast City Hall's most controversial characters. After Raymond's murder I bumped into Pootsy one day at the bottom of my street while out for a walk. My route took me past Mark Haddock's men sitting outside a pub. I deliberately walked past them and Pootsy walked with me past the UVF rabble. Not one of them spoke to us. Many people didn't like Pootsy, but I always got on well with him as he spoke his mind.

A small percentage of the Yard workforce was Catholic. They were often subjected to sectarian graffiti and threats scrawled on the toilet walls. Some decided to leave while others braved it out. It must have been extremely stressful for them and their families, not knowing if they would come home alive or dead. Many of the stagers were paramilitaries, some serving prison time for their activities. They strutted around like hard men and their tea huts were bedecked with loyalist flags and emblems. I had some friends among them. Some of my best friends in the Yard, who were welders like me, were 'connected', yet I never had a problem with them.

Over the years at the Yard I was involved in many fights with the UVF and the UDA, but none of these ever took place at work. My street fights became common knowledge among the workforce, but I never once came under any threat. However, that changed following Raymond's murder when graffiti appeared in the toilets stating: 'RIP Raymond McCord. Dead Man Walking', with drawings of bullets going into a head with my name on it. The messages sent by these brave UVF men of course left no name or a forwarding number for me. The Yard accepted me for not being 'connected', but there were times when I would have problems outside work with those who were.

In the early days of the Troubles the paramilitaries used the skills of its men to make guns in the shipyard. Officially the management knew nothing about this; unofficially there were managers, foremen and workers who between them helped to supply the paramilitaries with home-made hand

and machine guns constructed using shipyard machinery and secretly stored on the sprawling complex. Workshop managers knew better than to report these activities to the security forces. I never saw a gun being made; nor did most of the workers.

The Yard had its own football team called the Welders. My late, great mate Geordie Simpson and I had many a drink in the social club where we argued just for the hell of it. But no better friend could I have asked for, and after Raymond's murder he always stuck by me. Many UVF men drank in the club and would turn their back on me when I walked in, but not Geordie. My only regret is that he didn't live long enough to hear how the police had colluded in young Raymond's murder. He was so looking forward to the publication of the Police Ombudsman's report.

The Welders team under 'Tucker' Docherty were a great bunch of lads. He called it 'Tucker's team' when we won and the Welders when we lost. Some of my best Yard friends played on the team including Ronnie Stitt. I remember going to Geordie Simpson's funeral in the Braniel estate in east Belfast. I had been 'advised' by people connected to the Red Hand Commando (RHC) paramilitary group not to attend. Geordie's coffin was being removed from his father's house when I arrived with my son Gareth. Jaws dropped on the faces of UVF and RHC members when they saw us. The look on their faces was a treat; I'm sure Geordie was having a good laugh to himself. Ronnie Stitt didn't give a damn about the paramilitaries and walked over to me, shook my hand and walked with us. Ronnie was a real man and a true friend for what he did that day. The people who tried to stop me that day were friends of the late David Ervine, yet they had no objections to Gerry Adams attending his funeral in January 2007. It showed the depth of hatred the paramilitaries had for me, but we sent a message to the UVF that day: you don't scare us.

I also worked for four or five years at Mackies foundry on the Springfield Road in west Belfast. During the war years it made artillery shells and in later years it made world renowned textile machinery, employing 8,000 men and women until it went bust in 1999. It was situated in a mainly nationalist/republican area, but the workforce was predominantly Protestant. At the height of the Troubles workers were attacked by Catholic mobs as they headed home.

I worked in the maintenance squad under the watchful eye of Bertie Campbell, a crabby foreman. Bertie was a tough guy in his day, and he could still put the fear of God into us. He was a nightmare to work with. But I never once saw a job beat him. Bertie treated everyone the same and he had no favourites. One of our gang, who later became a senior loyalist paramilitary, was terrified of Bertie and would never dare miss a day or turn up late for work after a night on the beer. On his last day before retirement Bertie decided to tell each of his men what he thought of them. His words, as colourful as you could get, were unprintable. He tore strips off one guy, saying he was the 'laziest, lying bastard' he had ever come across. His old friend replied: 'You didn't really mean that, did you, Bertie?' The words were hardly out before Bertie launched into another tirade of abuse. I liked old Bertie. He was a fair boss.

One Mackies worker was a member of the notorious Shankill Butchers, the blood-thirsty UVF gang led by Lenny Murphy who abducted Catholics from the streets and slit their throats and mutilated their bodies with large butcher's knives. Murphy was later shot dead by two IRA gunmen in 1982. It was rumoured he was set up by UDA gangster and police informant Jim Craig, who saw Murphy as a rival to his money-spinning rackets.

At Mackies I supplemented my wages with a little scheme on the side. Every Friday I held a raffle and I would go around the workshops selling tickets. There were good prizes to be won — televisions, hi-fi systems, cameras etc. We would gather in a large workshop at dinner time when the tickets were drawn. If someone I didn't like had a winning ticket, I would call out a different number. Somebody went home on a Friday night with something new for the house and I went home with a few extra quid in my pocket.

Selling raffle tickets was against company rules, but that didn't stop me. One day I was at a meeting between the trade union and the management. The managing director was seated at one end of the table and I was at the other end in my capacity as chairman of the shop stewards' committee, the most senior of the trade union officials. As the meeting started to discuss a rise in wages for the workforce, I pulled a small bag out of my overalls and took out a handful of expensive watches and pushed them up the table towards the managing director and his senior team. The room fell silent. When I saw that the watches didn't interest him, I started the formal business of future wage talks. The management had never experienced anything like that before in their lives, but it worked to my advantage because some of the bosses, including the personnel manager, got in touch with me later and asked me what else I had for sale. The personnel manager even began buying a raffle ticket on a Friday, despite company policy. When the time came for the union to send me on a course to England, the management must have heaved a sigh of relief.

As in the shipyard, the paramilitaries inside Mackies also used the engineering equipment to make guns, firstly 'zip' guns which fired a single round and then machine guns. I remember a UDA man from the Shankill Road opening his locker and seeing guns inside. It wasn't my business and as long as the paramilitaries left me, my family and my friends alone, there would be no problems with me.

With Mackies being situated in a republican area, there was always a danger to the workforce. One manager was ambushed at a pelican crossing when he allowed a woman to cross the road before him. When he stopped, an IRA gunman shot him, but though seriously wounded he was still able to drive on. Years later he told me that a Mackies worker had set him up for assassination. The worker was a man who had once complained to me about the flying of the Union flags. He was later convicted of making bombs.

I had many good workers on the shop floor and one man I knew lived on the nearby Falls Road. He was a member of the Official IRA, a 'Stickie', who had the reputation for being a tough guy and who also hated the Provos. Most times the Provos and the Stickies wouldn't talk to each other; sometimes a Stickie would call a Provo a 'monkey'.

The Stickie one day asked me to give him a lift to his drinking club. As I was parking the car outside the club, I noticed a group of men sitting outside at the tables drinking. To my surprise, the Stickie told them to watch my car and to make sure nobody went near it. I was nervous going into the club in spite of his assurance that I would not be harmed. As he called for a drink for me, I overheard another drinker talking about a shooting that had just happened. The British Army had shot someone and as a Protestant drinking in a club in a strongly republican area I was more than just a bit concerned. The barman told the man there was to be no more talk about the shooting. I believe the barman knew I was a Protestant. I finished my drink, said goodbye and was about to open the door when one of the customers told us not to go out as there was an RUC checkpoint down the road. He told me to go up the Shankill Road to avoid the checkpoint. They must have known all along I was a Protestant.

We sometimes worked weekends and on a Sunday we would finish at lunchtime and head to a nearby Catholic-owned pub for a drink. One Sunday our foreman Bertie Campbell sent me and two others to repair company railings up the street which had been knocked down by joyriders. Several men approached us and told us they were taking our equipment and our electric truck which we used to carry our oxy-acetylene tanks. My two workmates, one of whom was a loyalist paramilitary, looked at me to see what I was going to do. I told the thugs they were not getting any of our equipment. As quick as a flash my workmates fled and I was left on my own. I quickly brokered a deal and sold them the equipment for £90. When I returned I told Bertie that the truck and our equipment had been taken. It was a profitable afternoon's work and I was the one smiling all the way to the bank.

I wish now that I hadn't worked those weekends because I missed out on my boys growing up. It was only when they were older that I realised how much more time I should have spent with them in their younger years. Hindsight is a wonderful thing, but it is too late now. You cannot turn back the clock. But in the end the shipyard and the foundry put a roof over our heads and food on the table.

6.
Young Raymond is Born

I can remember the day my first child came into the world almost like it was yesterday. Vivienne and I both shed tears of joy as it was such a special day. I was just a month away from my 21st birthday and Vivienne was a beautiful 19-year-old teenager. We married on 16 March 1973 and spent our honeymoon in England, even contemplating staying there to start a new life away from the Troubles. We decided to go back to Belfast and briefly stayed with my parents.

I was so happy when Vivienne told me she was pregnant with our first child. Raymond Christopher McCord was born on 24 November 1974 in the Jubilee maternity unit at Belfast City Hospital. Vivienne looked so proud with Raymond in her arms. The province was at a standstill because of the Ulster Workers' Council strike. We were living in our new home, a two-bedroom flat at Glenbane Avenue in Rathcoole. We decorated the spare room for Raymond and bought him a cot. Vivienne was admitted to hospital and I didn't realise how long I would have to wait for the birth. I kept ringing the hospital until one of the nurses told me it was time and I rushed from the house as quickly as I could. I declined a nurse's offer to put on a green gown and mask before going into the labour ward. I would have fainted at the sight of Vivienne giving birth and decided to wait in the corridor. Vivienne rightly called me a big coward. That afternoon Raymond Christopher was born, tipping the scales at 8 lb 3 oz. I knew he was going to bring us happiness. Relatives and friends called at our home and I was as proud as could be.

On Raymond's first Friday night home, our coalman Billy called looking for his money. He looked into the carry cot and put some money beside Raymond. I grabbed my shoes and went out to 'wet Raymond's head'. We jumped into Billy's car and he took me to the local UDA club in Rathcoole. Even then there was no love lost between the UDA and me. Billy bought a crate of beer which we polished off quickly and then we headed home.

Vivienne and Raymond were in perfect health and we were one happy family. Raymond's beaming smile lifted my spirits when I came home from work. After tea I would do the DIY work at night while Vivienne told me about her day. After his night feed Raymond slept all night, just like his mother. He was an easy child to bring up and never upset anyone, including us.

As the months passed, we moved his cot into his own room. One night when Vivienne was out, I decided to look in on Raymond. I gently opened the door and peered in. He was standing up with a big smile and a look that said: did you think I didn't hear you, daddy? I took him into the living room and we played on the floor together. After a while I put him back into his cot and he fell asleep. I never told Vivienne. I was having my private time with him as he was in bed most nights before I came home.

We bought him a musical train which he loved and played to his heart's content. When he was eight months old we all went to Butlin's Holiday Camp at Mosney in the Republic of Ireland. It was our first proper holiday since we got married and we were like a pair of excited children on the train. We were given a small but basic chalet room which had a double bed and a cot. At night the Red Coats who worked for Butlin's put on shows for the adults and provided a baby-sitting service. One day the Red Coats let us go to dinner while they looked after Raymond. After the meal we called to collect him. To our horror he was missing. We panicked and we had everyone looking for him. We immediately thought someone had snatched him, but to our relief we found him sleeping under some cushions in a corner. Never again would we go without him.

Despite the scare we relaxed and recharged our batteries. One cabaret night we met a nice Catholic couple from the New Lodge Road in Belfast. While we sat watching the show, a man came over and asked me my name and my religion. My Catholic friend recognised him and knew he was looking for a fight. The troublemaker told me his brother, who was sitting at another table with his mates, was going to 'do' me. A massive fight broke out and Butlin's sent for the local Guards. The place was like a bomb site and one of those who threatened me was lying cut and bloodied. The following morning we heard a crowd of young Belfast lads had smashed up some of the chalets, forcing some families to leave.

Vivienne entered Raymond and me for a father and son competition and we all had to parade on stage before a panel of judges. Some of the fathers and sons were dressed identically; I wore a pair of jeans and a T-shirt and young Raymond was in his baby clothes. We finished in second place and our prize was an engraved medal and photograph. That medal is always with me for I believe young Raymond is watching over me and hasn't failed me yet. I once gave it to my son Gareth when he went to Iraq to work, and it brought him back safe and sound.

When Raymond's first birthday came we made it special with balloons, buns, sweets and a birthday cake. Our house was packed with people wishing him a happy birthday.

When he started at Abbots Cross Primary School, young Raymond didn't have far to walk and Vivienne turned him out neat and tidy. Our eldest boy was taking his first steps in life and making his first friends. He was just a few years old when we moved to Rathfern. At the side of our new home was a football pitch where we kicked a ball about. When he was 2, Vivienne and I went on our first foreign holiday to Spain. My sister Jean looked after him. When we came home I sneaked up to Jean's house to collect him. But when he saw me he ran towards me and I gave him a big hug and a kiss. Vivienne and Raymond smothered each other and Vivienne's face showed how much she loved and missed him. Raymond was so happy to see his mum again.

Before we knew it young Raymond was starting secondary school. His younger brother Gareth was born in 1977 and Raymond loved him. The pair had a lot in common — big smiles, brotherly love and a great outpouring of affection. Gareth was a little devil. No one ever knocked our front door to complain about young Raymond, but loveable Gareth made up for that. He wanted to fight with everyone — neighbours, children and even his teachers. Gareth's first primary school report stated: 'Very likeable child but at times needs a firm hand.' His wife Debra, with whom he has two children, Dylan Raymond and Leah, is now his 'firm hand'. I remember Gareth's face when Vivienne and I split up. I feel bad about making him unhappy. I am not proud of what I did and I would do nothing to hurt my sons, but it felt like the right thing to do at the time. I'm sorry about my marriage breakdown, but it was a private matter and I hope it's the only time I let my sons down.

Our third son Glenn looks like Raymond and is quiet like him. All three loved football, but Glenn is our star who should really be playing in England. He represented Northern Ireland at schoolboy and youth international level and has many medals and caps to his credit. He and his lovely girlfriend Jacqueline have a beautiful baby daughter Nicole who is Glenn's double.

Gareth and Glenn shared a room with posters of their favourite teams and players adorning the walls. Raymond had his own room. His walls were covered with posters of planes. He was fascinated with them and although he loved football, aeroplanes took priority. Once while playing centre forward for Hopefield, he almost got into trouble when he stopped to watch a plane overhead while the ball was crossed to him.

At night Raymond was up in his room listening to a small radio on which he could listen to pilots talking as it was tuned into their waveband. He would take it downstairs in case he missed something. His bedroom had become his own private cockpit where he would spend hours dreaming about being a pilot. Once he asked me to take him to Newtownards to watch the annual air show. I gave him some money, dropped him off and collected him later. He just wanted to spend time on his own watching the planes. I think he decided in his teens that he wanted to join the RAF and it was no surprise when he eventually did. At that time he was living with me as Vivienne and I had separated. He loved his mum, but he thought he would get away with more living with me. We had a special bond and in his eyes I could do no wrong. I moved to a flat in Rathcoole, a bachelor pad with two bedrooms.

Raymond joined the RAF on 10 December 1991 aged 17. I was a proud father that day watching him being sworn in at RAF Aldergrove. It was a proud day for Raymond as it was something he had always wanted to do. He joined as an aerospace systems operator and rose to the rank of senior aircraftman. He served in the Falkland Islands and I remember him telling me he would be able to save plenty of money as there was nothing to do there. Nevertheless he still came home penniless. He spent his wages as soon as he got paid just to have a good time. When he returned from the Falklands, he found out that his RAF girlfriend had been seeing another bloke. He didn't tell me, but somehow his mum knew and she told me. I bought him a plane ticket home and he met up with a few of his mates and was soon back to his old self.

He never had a shortage of girlfriends and they never had a bad word to say about him. Young Raymond thought of himself as a bit of a Casanova. With one particular girl he stayed overnight at her home when her mum and dad were away for the weekend. I knew nothing about it. If her father had found out he would have given him a right hiding. One St Patrick's Day I was in a Belfast city centre pub with a few mates having a laugh and a Guinness. Two girls were standing near me talking and one asked me if I remembered her. I didn't, but she said she had been in my house in York Road with Raymond, but only for a few minutes. That night I spoke to the girl for about an hour about Raymond and she had nothing but nice things to say about him. The girl was from Andersonstown in west Belfast, a republican stronghold. Raymond wouldn't hesitate to go out with a Catholic girl. The girl said they had been to each other's houses a few times. Since his murder I have met a few of his former girlfriends and I could listen to them all day. It still made him feel alive in my heart.

Raymond made many good friends in the RAF. One was a Liverpool lad, Wayne. His mum and dad treated Raymond like a son whenever he stayed with them. Wayne has never forgotten Raymond and each year on his anniversary he sends a very expensive floral display to Raymond's mum to put on his grave. He has been a true friend to our son.

Raymond's trips home usually cost me money as he was always broke, but like any father I just wanted to make sure he was happy. My house was where he could put his head down and between my house and his mum's he knew he would be well fed and spoiled rotten. But I was glad I never had to make him dinner because he was the pickiest eater you could ever meet. Vivienne knew what he liked and that was what she put in front of him.

Before Raymond joined the RAF and while he was living with me, the UDA kicked in the door of my Rathcoole home which was empty at the time. I saw who was involved when I pulled up just as they were leaving. The only damage was a broken front door lock. I was concerned for my son's safety and left him with a close friend Rab Foster, where he and his wife Sally would look after him until I sorted out the problem. I drove to the ringleader's second-floor flat, kicked in his door but there was no one at home. I opened a front window and threw out whatever would fit through the opening. I threw out his settee, his television, along with his bed and other furniture which landed on the garden below. As I was getting into my car, startled neighbours came out on hearing the commotion, and I told them to let the so-called UDA hard man know that I had emptied his flat. I headed off to the pub to reward myself with a pint of Guinness for a good day's work. The UDA never retaliated. My attitude was very simple: if they annoyed me, then I would pay them a visit to their own homes with no balaclavas, no baseball bats, just good old-fashioned street justice. Raymond was safe with Rab and Sally. She spoiled him, giving him breakfast in bed. Poor Rab told me he had to go to the shops with a list for food Sally wanted and it was all for Raymond. To make matters worse she was also giving my son pocket money! Sally and Rab were true friends and I have never forgotten their kindness and generosity towards my son.

After four years in the RAF, Raymond finally came home and later got himself a two-bedroomed house a few streets from me. As usual he was penniless and I helped him buy household goods and furniture. We measured his living room and then headed off to buy a roll of carpet for it. Glenn was living with me but Raymond was in my house every day raiding the kitchen. I didn't really mind.

The police called at my house one Saturday morning in 1997 to say Raymond had been arrested and would be appearing in court that morning. I was totally stunned. I raced down to Belfast Magistrates Court and after a few minutes young Raymond appeared in the dock charged with possession of cannabis. He had a look of shame on his face because he knew I hated drugs. The magistrate remanded him in custody, but I was allowed to see him for five minutes before he was taken to jail. He didn't know what to say to me, but he was my son and I would stick by him, visiting him several times in jail.

Later, I found out that the drugs belonged to Mount Vernon UVF, but finding out who organised the drug run would take a bit longer. Raymond eventually got bail and, as part of the conditions, he had to report regularly to the police and live outside the area. He finally got himself a full-time job with a former RAF man who had his own business. I thought this would keep him out of trouble, but weeks before he was murdered he told me the UVF were going to shoot him in the leg, a so-called 'punishment shooting', over the drugs. I told him no one would be shooting him. I have asked myself a thousand times since why I didn't see the danger he was facing and why I didn't do more to protect him.

Shortly before his murder he asked for £20 to go for a night out. For the first time I refused him and said he wouldn't have much left out of his social security money once he paid me back. He accepted that without any argument because I was his dad and he had to take my word. That is why I know my son was not a drug dealer because he was always broke. He was being used by UVF elements.

During his last week alive I went with Raymond to court to get his bail conditions changed as he had started work in Lisburn. Outside the court we said our goodbyes and off he walked to Central Station to catch his train to Lisburn. That was to be the last time I would see young Raymond alive.

7.
We've Found your Son's Body Murdered

I was in no real danger from the UDA unless I was seen in Rathcoole where the local unit would still have tried to kill me. I was always careful not to stay too long in the estate as it would have given them time to put a team together to kill me. Even though the UDA still presented a real threat to my life, I continued to visit friends in the estate whom I had grown up with years before. The sight of me driving into Rathcoole got up the noses of the local UDA leaders, which pleased me no end. I was determined that a bunch of thugs who hid behind the flag of an organisation would not dictate to me where I could go. Those same thugs wouldn't have dared even look at me if they were on their own.

But just because the UDA couldn't get to me, it didn't stop them turning their attention towards my sons. My second boy Gareth bore the brunt of their attacks and on several occasions he and his friends were set upon by UDA thugs. These louts didn't care that he didn't live with me or that he was only 18 years of age. As far as they were concerned he was a McCord and that was enough.

One Saturday night in Belfast city centre a carload of

Rathcoole UDA men followed Gareth and one of his mates. Earlier in the evening the UDA team had spotted them in a nightclub and threatened them before the UDA gang were evicted by the doormen. Gareth thought that was the end of the matter. He looked upon them as cowardly thugs. But what Gareth didn't know was that the UDA were about to step up to a new and more dangerous level. At closing time Gareth and his friend left the nightclub and went into the city centre in search of a taxi to take them home. The UDA team followed them in a car. Suddenly they jumped from their car armed with baseball bats and launched a vicious attack on my boy and his friend. Gareth sustained severe bruising and cuts while his mate suffered a fractured skull. True to form, Gareth and his friend fought back. Had they not done so, I believe their injuries would have been much more severe, possibly even life threatening. The UDA in Rathcoole obviously believed that Gareth would lie down and not fight back against the cowardly thugs. But the UDA didn't know my Gareth and he reported it to the RUC.

As part of the investigation, a number of arrests were made and the case against them eventually came to court. Four of them pleaded guilty to the assault. For some reason neither the police nor the lawyer for the Director of Public Prosecutions (DPP) office mentioned the fact that those in the dock had used baseball bats in the attack. Not one of them was given a custodial sentence. Instead they walked from the court with a slap on the wrist and a fine. Gareth and I sat in the court throughout the proceedings and witnessed first hand how justice was meted out to a bunch of paramilitary gangsters. When the case was over, the police asked us to wait behind in court until the UDA men and their cohorts had left, as the RUC could not guarantee our safety. If it hadn't been more serious it would have been laughable.

Here was the force of law and order in Northern Ireland telling us to stay behind in a court building because they couldn't protect us from a bunch of thugs. Against the advice of the police, Gareth and I walked out past the UDA mob. It was they who were forced to stay behind in the court building. Gareth had the right attitude, to face down his attackers and not be afraid of them. A bully always hates to be confronted and will always back down. I was very proud of my son, but I also knew that we were cooking up another storm with the UDA. However, we would not be running away to hide.

My sons had been on the receiving end of previous attacks by the UDA while they were living in the Rathfern estate. Their home was attacked three nights in a row and on the last night shots were fired at the house. Gareth, who was still only a teenager, chased after the gunmen with a poker in his hand. My sons were being attacked by grown men, and yet during all this intimidation and attempts on my family's lives no one came to our aid. We stood alone to defend ourselves and our property but we were not afraid. In fact the Rathcoole UDA men were having many a sleepless night fearing a visit. The trouble between the UDA and myself increased and when I crossed paths with those who were involved in attacks on my sons or their home, I dealt with them in my own way. I have never professed to be an angel, but I had to protect my family as the police adopted the attitude of taking the easy option and arrested me instead of those paramilitaries who were intimidating my family. I was left with no choice but to defend my family and put the fear of God into those who were carrying out the attacks and the armchair generals who gave the orders.

At times there was no friction between me and the UDA, but I was always on my guard as I knew trouble was never too far from the surface. My youngest son Glenn was still at secondary school when the local UDA brigadier from Rathcoole verbally abused him outside the school gates. Glenn was coming out of school to get into a bus when the brigadier (I will call him 'H') started abusing Glenn from the safety of his car. Glenn was just a child and was quite scared. When he told me what happened, I decided to pay 'H' a visit. The following day I was sitting in my car waiting for Glenn when I spotted the brave brigadier who got his kicks from intimidating young boys. I got out of my car and walked towards him. He was sitting in his car with his wife waiting to collect their daughter. As soon as he spotted me he wound up his windows and locked the doors. I told him to get out of the car, but he refused. As he sat cowering behind the steering wheel, I shouted a few home truths at him through the closed window. Over the next few weeks when I went to collect Glenn, there was no sign of the brigadier. He wasn't the tough man he thought he was. Eventually the UDA expelled him for stealing money from the organisation's coffers. Today he is left without a friend in the world.

UDA intimidation of my family took a sinister new twist when they tried to murder a friend. Glenn was going out with a girl in Rathfern and one night the UDA called to her home. Masked and armed men warned her father not to let me across his door, or else. This man was a very quiet individual and, unlike myself, had never had any trouble with the paramilitaries. After the gunmen left and with the warning still ringing in his ears, the man phoned me and told me what had happened. For the sake of his family's safety I decided to stay away from his house. But that didn't stop the UDA trying to kill him. One night he and his wife were going up to bed when gunmen kicked in his front door. The couple ran into a bedroom and held the door shut tight fearing for their lives. The gunmen fired shotgun blasts through the door and seriously wounded my friend. When the gunmen fled, it was left to his terrified wife to ring for an ambulance, the police and me.

By the time I arrived my friend was already on his way to the hospital and his house cordoned off by the police. Not far from the police tape several local UDA men were standing. I made quite sure they saw me and I made it obvious that I had seen them too. My friend's only crime was that he was a mate and that my son was going out with his daughter. For some reason known only to the police, the investigating officers were more concerned about how often he would have been with me rather than concerning themselves with those behind the attempt on his life. No one has ever been charged with the attempted murder of my friend, even though the identity of the gunmen was known within a matter of hours of the shooting. This did not surprise me. As a result of the murder bid, my friend nearly lost an arm and had to move house. Our only consolation over the attempted murder was that the gunman who fired the shots was later shot on two separate occasions. I can honestly say he got very little sympathy from me. No one has ever been charged with those two shootings either.

With Glenn living with me in York Road and away from Rathfern, things started to settle down. It was a weight off my mind having him under my roof. Gareth was living with his girlfriend and Raymond had a house around the corner from me. There hadn't been any serious trouble between me or my sons with the UDA in Rathcoole. In fact Raymond was in Rathcoole a lot as he still had quite a few friends living in the estate. With Raymond out on bail and working hard at his new job, life was starting to return to normal. That week in November 1997 I thought was the start of better things for young Raymond. I was not to know it would turn out to be the worst of our lives. Every Saturday afternoon I would shower and change and head into Belfast city centre. Even though I was still under threat from the UDA, I would still drink in the same pub every week, the Monico, just off High Street. The pub was packed every Saturday afternoon with punters who flitted between the bookies next door and the afternoon shoppers who called in for a quiet drink. By 6 p.m. the atmosphere was lively and friendly as a music group started to entertain us. For a change I decided not to go out that Saturday, 8 November. Instead I stayed indoors at my small house in Seaview Street, next door to York Road RUC Station, and had a few beers. Young Raymond wouldn't have called to see me as he probably thought I was out for my regular Saturday afternoon drink.

As usual I was up early on Sunday morning and headed out. I was wearing my poppy as it was Remembrance Sunday, 9 November, the day when people in Northern Ireland and mainland Britain remembered those who fought and died for their country through different wars. When I see loyalist paramilitaries walking on Remembrance Sunday I wonder what the men of the regular army, the Royal Navy and the Royal Air Force from past wars would think of them. Like me, they would probably be disgusted at seeing sectarian killers, drug dealers and extortionists laying wreaths at war memorials. It is grotesque that these paramilitaries believe they in some way belong to honourable armies or associations.

Around 5 p.m. there was a knock at my front door. My first thought was that it was probably young Raymond as Glenn was out and he had his own front door key. I opened the door and there were two men dressed in suits standing on my doorstep. They identified themselves as police officers and I brought them into the house to the kitchen. I initially thought it was something to do with the UDA as the police were never too slow in following up any complaint the UDA made against me. If they weren't here to question me about alleged assaults on UDA men or even a gun attack on them, I thought, what else were they in my house for? One of the officers spoke: 'Mr McCord, your son's body has been found. . . .' That's all I remember. I started to shout and scream, but to this day I don't know what I said. It all happened so suddenly. Then the police were gone. I went into the living room, sat down and cried. I still can't describe my feelings. I was thinking, how could my son Raymond be dead, murdered? When reality hit home that this was not a sick joke and I wasn't having a nightmare, I was faced with the hardest thing I had ever done in my life — to tell Vivienne, Gareth and Glenn the heartbreaking news. To this day I will never forget the look on their faces. They couldn't believe it. No one could. They could have accepted it more easily if it had been me because of all the trouble I had had over the years with the paramilitaries. But not our son. For the first time in my life I realised what a broken heart felt like. The tears just wouldn't stop and neither would the pain. I truly wished it was me they had killed and not young Raymond. He had his whole life in front of him at 22 years of age. Why not me?

There are parts of that Remembrance Sunday which are still a blur. It is almost as if I had a blackout and pieces of the jigsaw are missing. I remember asking a friend to go and tell my mother the bad news. It broke her heart. She loved all my sons, but young Raymond was her favourite. I also remember making a few phone calls to other family members and friends to tell them that Raymond had been murdered. That evening some relatives and friends called round to comfort me. I don't honestly remember what was said, or who said what. It is all still very fuzzy in my head.

The police phoned me later to say that I needed to go to the mortuary at Foster Green Hospital in south Belfast to make a formal identification of young Raymond's body. It was the start of another nightmare thinking about how I could bring myself to identify his remains. Two of my friends and Glenn came with me. During the whole journey across the city from north to south Belfast, my stomach was churning and flipping over inside. I felt sick to the pit of my stomach. We arrived at the mortuary and waited for the police. The wait seemed like an eternity. When the police officers eventually arrived, they accompanied me into the mortuary building to meet the morgue attendant. It was at this point that the attendant told me I couldn't see young Raymond due to the severity of his injuries. On the one hand I was glad; on the other I just felt sick. Even the police agreed with the attendant's advice that I should not go in and see my son. I just wanted to get away as far as possible from that place. My lovely son was dead and I couldn't even see him.

When we arrived back home a steady stream of people called at my door. Catholics from west Belfast and the Ardoyne in north Belfast were among those who came to express their sympathies. Others sent flowers.

Two days before he was buried, I received a phone call from a local funeral director to say that the mortuary had released Raymond's body and that I could now make arrangements for the funeral. I went to the funeral director's and was shown into a room where Raymond's coffin was placed. The coffin was closed so I asked an assistant to open the coffin lid very slightly. I didn't want to see his face because I wanted to remember him just the way he was the last time I saw him. The assistant opened the lid and called me back into the room. I held my son's hand for the last time and spoke to him as the tears ran down my face. I told him I loved him, that I didn't want him to go away and I promised him justice no matter what. When the assistant came back, I stood up, pulled myself together and left the room. It was a very difficult moment as it would be the last time I would ever see him. All I have of him are memories but they are good memories. A few hours later Raymond was brought home to his mum's house. Vivienne was already heartbroken at losing Raymond and I wondered how she would cope with him laid out in her front room in the closed coffin. I tried to be strong for my family, but believe me it was hard.

Nobody, not even Vivienne, ever knew that I used to leave her house just to cry on my own. I cried many times before the funeral; I have cried many times since, and to this day I still do. The whole time Raymond's coffin was at his mum's, Gareth and Glenn were always at his side. It broke my heart looking at them. Every waking minute of the day, all I could think of was Raymond and who had killed him. Before he was buried, Ulster Television interviewed me about his murder and I said that I wished it had been me, that it should have been me and not him lying in a coffin. He was just another innocent victim. I was the one who had fought with the paramilitaries all my adult life, sometimes working outside the law to get justice. Raymond didn't.

On Friday, 14 November 1997, five days after his body was found bludgeoned to death at Ballyduff quarry on the northern outskirts of Belfast, we held a funeral service for Raymond. A very large crowd turned up to pay their respects, which was heart warming for my family as it showed us that he was a popular young man. The funeral service is still very hazy as I was still coming to terms with what had happened to Raymond. I now know that some of those who were involved in his killing also attended. If I had known that then, they would have been burying two more people that day as I would have killed them with my bare hands. But the devil looks after his own, as I have since found out. UVF men came up to me offering me support, guns and promises. Even their brigadier, Rab Warnock, sent a message of support as he was unable to attend the funeral. I now know why, because like some of the UVF who attended the funeral, Warnock knew what had happened to my son as it was men under his command who had killed him.

Even in death the UDA would not let their feud with me rest. A female relative of UDA brigadier John 'Grug' Gregg also attended the funeral as she was fond of young Raymond. When Grug found out, he gave her terrible abuse. He was still bitter towards me after I beat him to a pulp in his local bar and he was shown up to be nothing more than a bully.

I have no memory of what hymns were sung at the funeral service. The church was packed and I can't remember who was sitting beside whom in the church. I don't remember if I was sitting beside Gareth or Glenn or Vivienne. I do remember that the minister spoke well of Raymond. When we came out of the church, I don't know how I held myself together to carry young Raymond's coffin on my shoulder. I probably found the inner strength because I didn't want to let Vivienne or my other sons down. If I had broken down, so would they. Gareth was 20 and Glenn was only 15 years old, but that day they grew quickly into men. As we stood at the graveside in Carnmoney Cemetery just outside Belfast, I will never forget the looks on their young faces when their older brother's coffin was lowered into the ground. The pain and the hurt was etched across their faces. God only knows what was going through their minds. It was heartbreaking to watch. As a father, I felt their pain and hurt and it is something I will take to my grave. Looking at my sons' tortured faces was all the determination I needed to find out who killed their brother. I made a vow that day that I would leave no stone unturned to find out who was responsible. No one was going to get away with this murder. If I could have wished for something bad on those who killed him, it was for one of them to lose a child of their own, for there is no pain like it.

After paying our last respects in the cemetery, we headed back to Vivienne's house. I never felt an atmosphere like it in my life, even though so many people had come back to her house. It was lifeless. It felt like all our souls had been ripped out. I found it so hard to believe that Raymond was gone.

A short time after the funeral I bumped into a senior republican from Belfast who expressed his sympathy to my family and me. He said he wanted to attend young Raymond's funeral but in the end decided against it. I told him he should have come along as nobody would have said a word to him. His political views and mine were totally different, but I understood that he wanted to show me respect. I've never forgotten that.

In the wake of young Raymond's murder, all I wanted to do was find out who murdered him, who was involved and who ordered it, and I was convinced that the UDA's south east Antrim brigade had killed him as part of its feud with my family and me. The brigadier was the one I wanted. I went looking for the head of that organisation's snake to get answers. He owned a pub, so I rang it and one of his workers, a woman, answered. I gave her a message to give to the brigadier. It was not long after this, and possibly the first time in the organisation's blood-filled history, that the UDA in south east Antrim issued a statement concerning my son's murder. It said in effect that although in the past they had

had problems with the McCord family, these were now at an end, and that south east Antrim UDA had had nothing to do with my son's murder. The brigadier at that time was a worried man and he had every right to be. He lived in my old stomping ground of Rathcoole and he knew that he would not be safe from me if I found out his men had been involved. The statement was issued as much for his benefit as it was for my family's.

Luckily for this brigadier the police informed me the day before Raymond's funeral that they were planning to make a number of arrests. The RUC didn't enlighten me as to who was going to be arrested, but as I have since discovered, the police received information in the days after my son's murder pinpointing who was involved and who gave the orders. The murder was in fact carried out by the UVF's 3rd battalion of Mount Vernon and Shore Road. Yet it wasn't until 19 November, a full ten days after the murder, that a number of people were arrested. The police had received information that Mark Haddock, the commanding officer of Mount Vernon UVF, had directly ordered my son's murder from his prison cell, yet he was not arrested until a staggering fourteen weeks later. Could the police have acted more quickly? I believe so, because fourteen weeks is a long time to wait to arrest a suspect who was already in prison for a UVF attack on the Golden Hind pub in Portadown, Co. Armagh. But when the suspect was Mark Haddock, who I later discovered was a highly paid RUC Special Branch informant, the normal rules of justice did not apply. The Special Branch had a policy to protect Haddock no matter what.

From the earliest days of the investigation, the RUC knew who murdered my son. As far as my family and I were concerned, little or nothing was being done to bring those responsible to justice. From a family point of view the investigation lacked leadership, direction and a will to get the perpetrators. After the start of the investigation, the RUC practically ignored my family and me. No one would tell us what was going on. Did the RUC think that because a registered police informant was involved in my son's murder, he was immune from prosecution and that the investigation would be hushed up and I would go away quietly? How wrong they were. My motto is that if you believe in something, then go for it, win or lose, and I wasn't going to lose in proving who was involved.

I started to dig into the dark twilight world of the UVF looking for clues as to who was actually involved in my son's murder. I wanted to know too why they had killed young Raymond. One of my first ports of call was the home of John 'Bonzo' Bond. I knew Bond to be a member of the Mount Vernon UVF, who later went to prison after he was caught trying to extort money from an undercover policeman posing as a businessman. The night I arrived at his house in Mount Vernon, there was another man with him whom he introduced to me as 'Woody'. I had never seen or heard of Woody before. We said hello and I asked Bonzo when he had last seen my son. He said it was the previous Saturday when Raymond and he had gone to the Maze Prison to visit Raymond's friend, Darren Moore, in a car being driven by Stephen Logue. He said Raymond suggested going into Belfast that night for a drink, but Bonzo said he told my son that he wasn't feeling well and was going to have a quiet night at home. He told me that the last place he had seen young Raymond was when he and Stephen Logue dropped him off at a garage following the jail visit. Police later recovered close circuit television footage from the garage which showed my son there, and the officers also knew he walked to his home at Alexander Park Avenue which was only a few streets away.

Bonzo also assured me that night that if he found out anything about the murder he would let me know. During the meeting my son Gareth was sitting in my car outside Bonzo's house when a carload of the UVF appeared on the scene. Gareth knocked on the front door and told us of the new arrivals. Bonzo told me not to worry and that I was safe as the men outside were friends of his and Woody. Maybe they were there to protect Bonzo in case they thought something was going to happen to him. Only Bonzo can answer that question. As far as I was concerned, I didn't give a damn if they were for me or against me. All I knew was that if they got out of the car that night and said something nasty to me, they wouldn't be getting back into their car again. Gareth and I would have made sure of that. Maybe that was why they stayed in their car the whole time we were there.

Strangely, there were other UVF men in the street that night who approached me and offered me help, but I declined. Never in my life did I need paramilitaries to fight for me or my family. I told them that I alone would deal with whoever was behind young Raymond's murder. To this day that still applies and I only hope the police will one day convict those involved. At the time, I believed in the police and I never thought they would let my family down. I had clashed with the RUC many times in the past over a difference of opinion, none more so than in their failure to arrest UDA men who carried out attacks on Vivienne's home as well as attacks on Gareth. It was little wonder that sometimes I had to take the law into my own hands. I thought that on this occasion things would be different, that because they were dealing with a murder it would be only a matter of time before someone was charged. How naive I was. Little did I know that the leader of a UVF killer gang in north Belfast was in the pay of the RUC Special Branch. We were to find out later that Mount Vernon UVF was riddled with Special Branch informers who, like Mark Haddock, were able to kill at will without fear of prosecution. No one in the Protestant areas of north Belfast would have believed that the police were controlling such a dangerous gang of UVF men. When the RUC made arrests on 19 November, we were sure that someone would be charged, but our hopes soon faded when all the suspects were released without charge. Those arrested were all members of the UVF in Mount Vernon, so it was clear the RUC had ruled out UDA involvement and were focusing their investigation on the UVF, who were supposed to be on ceasefire since 1994.

As part of the planned raids, detectives arrested an inmate in the Maze Prison, Willie 'Mr Muscles' Young, who was in jail for possession of a firearm and who had been out on weekend parole when Raymond was murdered. He refused to answer any questions about the murder or his movements on that day. But what I found out to my amazement later was that neither the RUC nor the Prison Service had carried out a search of his cell for possible forensic evidence that could link him to the murder. Up until his arrest, I had never heard of Young and had never seen him. The Prison Service denied the police entry into his cell for a search. Bond and Stephen Logue were also arrested as they were with Raymond when he was last seen alive. While they were being questioned at Castlereagh Interrogation Centre, the main police custody suite in Belfast for interviewing terrorist suspects, the RUC were unable to find Logue's car. However, within hours of his release, the car was found burning not far from a police station in north Belfast. Yet no one had seen anyone setting it on fire.

Logue lived not far from me, but suddenly he moved out after his release and was given sanctuary in Mount Vernon. It was both foolish and careless of me to go into Mount Vernon to look for him, but I felt I had nothing to lose. I wasn't able to find where Logue was staying, but I knew I would be able to track him down to a local pub or club where he drank with Bond. The Saturday after his release I walked into a UVF pub, sat down at the bar counter beside three UVF members and ordered a pint. I asked the UVF men if Bonzo or Logue had been in. Two of the men, who were former prisoners, told me that I would be better off leaving the pub. I told them not to get involved or I would take it that they were siding with Bonzo and Logue. Their attitude changed and they offered to buy me a drink, but I refused. I waited for half an hour for Bonzo or Logue to turn up as this was where they drank every Saturday, but on this occasion they never showed their faces. Maybe they were too worried and scared in case I showed up and spoiled their party. I finished my pint and headed to a local social club near by. I was half expecting trouble so I left the car and walked.

The doormen at the club looked surprised to see me as I walked into the club and when I went into the main bar, everybody turned and looked. You could have heard a pin drop. I ordered a pint and asked the barman and the customers if they had seen Bonzo or Logue. It was no surprise that no one had. Next I went upstairs to the function room where a dance was taking place. I have never forgotten the looks on their faces when I walked in. They knew full well that I had come looking for those who had been involved in my son's murder. But Bonzo or Logue were not there either. They were hiding like rats, I thought. For a while I stayed in the bar waiting for the pair and during all that time none of the UVF men present, some of whom were from Mount Vernon, came near me. But if trouble had started, I would have lost and would probably have ended up like young

Raymond in a coffin if they had been able to get me outside. However, none of the Mount Vernon crew had the guts that night to throw the first punch. A relative came and picked me up and drove me the short distance to my Seaview Street home. On the way back I wondered what would have happened to Bond and Logue if they had turned up. At the very least they would have been seriously injured, maybe even ended up dead. Who knows?

The following morning a man arrived at my house wanting to speak to me. He introduced himself as Stephen Logue's father. He said he had heard I was looking for his son in connection with young Raymond's murder. I told him that was correct and when I caught up with him I would sort the problem out. Logue's father tried to convince me that his son had nothing to do with the murder, but I knew he was lying, and so did he. The conversation was very short and I advised him to leave my home and said: 'Tell your son I know he was involved in my son's murder and I will catch up with him.' As he left my home I told him on the front doorstep not to come back. He wisely took my advice and hasn't darkened my door since. I didn't really have a problem with Logue's father, but I knew that if he pushed matters he would be in very serious trouble. His son eventually moved out of north Belfast for the sake of his health.

Since young Raymond's murder my life had become hectic. It had been turned upside down, but I was determined to fulfil the promise I made Raymond as I held his hand in the coffin, that I would hunt down those who had killed him even if it took me the rest of my life. Three weeks later there were still so many unanswered questions surrounding his killing: what did happen to him that night in Ballyduff quarry? Did they murder him elsewhere and then dump his body at the quarry? How was he murdered? Who murdered him? Why did they murder him? The RUC were giving us no information regarding their progress in the murder investigation. No one can imagine how frustrating it was for us at the lack of information we were getting from the police. Even when the suspects were arrested, the officer in charge of the investigation kept us largely in the dark. Why, I asked, were they not telling us anything? It was so frustrating. I was asking more and more questions in the north Belfast and Newtownabbey areas. I felt no one was doing anything positive. Not long before the suspects were released, I discovered that the RUC were searching for Stephen Logue's car on suspicion that it was used to take my son to Ballyduff quarry. Through my own enquiries about his car I found out that it had been valeted since the murder, and where it had been cleaned. Unfortunately no one was able to find it before it was torched as it could have provided the police with forensic clues.

I decided to go to the Maze Prison and speak to Darren Moore who had been jailed for his part in the attack on the Golden Hind pub, and whom young Raymond had gone to visit that Saturday he was killed. I believed he would tell me anything he knew and I trusted him because he was Raymond's mate. My son had put a roof over his head when his parents kicked him out when they discovered he was in the UVF. So I thought with good reason that he would want to help catch those who had killed his friend. When I arrived at the visitors' room the adrenalin was pumping through my veins. As I waited for Moore to arrive, sitting across from me were the UVF chief of staff, his provost marshall Norman Sayers, and Rab Warnock, the UVF brigadier for south east Antrim who was convicted for terrorist crimes. At the time I didn't know who the UVF chief of staff was, but I recognised the other two. The short, stocky man approached me and whispered in my ear: 'There will be no cover-up in your son's murder.' I was later told that this man was John 'Bunter' Graham, the UVF chief of staff. I wanted to follow up this brief conversation and the UVF leadership, based on the Shankill Road in west Belfast, agreed to meet me. After listening to what I had to say, the UVF leadership decided to hold an inquiry into the murder. I actually believed it was going to get somewhere and would provide me with answers to my questions.

The visit with Moore was about to start. The prison officers opened a door and Darren Moore appeared. I could see he was nervous and I put that down to the fact that he was feeling bad over Raymond's murder. I asked him if he had heard anything and also warned him to be careful when talking to Mark Haddock. By then I had already received information that Haddock was a tout and was involved in Raymond's murder. Moore said he had been receiving treatment for shock and depression and was also taking medication since he heard about Raymond. But what he told me that day was a pack of lies, as I later discovered, and that no prison doctor had been treating him. When I left Moore that day, he told me that if he heard anything he would phone me. He also told me he had a gun hidden on the outside and when he got out there would be dead people on the streets for killing his mate. But Moore had been well schooled by his master, Mark Haddock, in the art of deception and deceit: make friends with your enemy, win over his trust, find out what he knows and then deal with him. This was a tactic Haddock had used on more than one occasion. After my visit Moore would have returned to the UVF's H-Block and told Haddock what I had said, and Haddock would have known that I knew he was a tout.

With Haddock's secret out of the bag, that he was an RUC

Special Branch informer, he had only one option open to him, and that was to silence me. He needed to protect his double life and so from his prison cell he hatched another plan to bump off another McCord — me. The following week I received a phone call around 11 o'clock one night from a UVF man who lived in Mount Vernon. It was a cold, wintry night outside. Expressing sympathy, he asked me if I wanted to come to his house for a beer or a cup of tea to take my mind off my son's murder. It sounded like a good offer as I was feeling depressed and at a very low point. But there was something not quite right about this late night call. When I declined his offer, he asked me to come over the following night instead. Again I said no, but I told him I looked forward to speaking with him at some other time. They thought they could lure me into a trap just like Raymond. To the man who made the call I say: I have a long memory.

To this day he has avoided me. Like me, he was a welder and we even worked on the same jobs together one time. It wasn't long after his late night call that he suddenly retired from his trade and I often wondered why. It appeared that certain individuals were trying to lure me into Mount Vernon at night on the pretext of wanting to express their sympathy, but I have no doubt that once in the estate I would never have left it alive. A young lad out to make a name for himself with the UVF would have been given a sawn-off shotgun to kill me. If he had succeeded, people loyal to Haddock and corrupt police officers would have put it down to a drugs dispute. Haddock thought he was smart, but he was not smart enough. He would need to be up early in the morning to catch me out. I was not going to fall for one of his tricks.

As usual, when people tried to set me up for a fall, I normally paid them a visit to let them explain themselves! As the weeks passed, those involved in Raymond's murder were known to be suffering from sleepless nights in their homes in Mount Vernon, Rathcoole and Monkstown, another estate on the outskirts of Belfast. They knew I would not rest until I got those responsible. It was widely rumoured at the time that I had been spotted in the early hours of the morning outside some of their homes. But they were only rumours. Some claimed I tried to get into their houses in the middle of the night. I wonder why.

During the weeks and months after young Raymond was murdered, the UVF was supposed to be conducting its own inquiry into the killing. The organisation's leadership had told me that if it was proved that Mark Haddock was working for the RUC, he would not come out of the Maze Prison alive. They were hollow words, and to my disgust I found out that the inquiry was a sham. Little did I know then that some of the UVF leadership were working for the same Special Branch department as Haddock. The UVF command structure was riddled with informants which went all the way to the top of the organisation to its chief of staff, John 'Bunter' Graham. I believe there were some honourable men involved in this inquiry, but the inquiry was suddenly stopped. They should be asking themselves who stopped it and why? Whoever stopped it was working for the Special Branch as it was in their interest to keep all their informants in place, even if they had been involved in murder. During one meeting at the UVF headquarters on the Shankill Road, the provost marshall to the brigade staff, Norman Sayers, who is now dead, told me that he believed me and that he wanted to shoot Bonzo Bond and Stephen Logue and have Willie Young and Mark Haddock dealt with in jail. He wanted them all dead as he had responsibility for all matters of internal discipline, but that strangely had been taken out of his hands by Graham. This contradicted everything Graham had told me at the Maze Prison, that there would be no cover-up of Raymond's murder. The dogs in the street knew who ordered his killing and who carried out those orders. The police also had intelligence and other information about those responsible for the murder, but nothing was happening as far as I could see.

I had a further meeting at the UVF headquarters which was attended by Norman Sayers, another senior UVF figure whom I will call 'Mr M', and Rab Warnock, the south east Antrim brigadier who was also Mark Haddock's boss. Warnock said my son had been a member of the UVF for only a few weeks and that he had put him out because he hadn't been properly 'schooled', whatever that meant. It went contrary to what David Ervine, the political spokesman for the UVF, had been telling the media about my son and his involvement with the UVF. I was told from the horse's mouth that at the time of his murder, Raymond was not a member of the UVF. During that meeting Warnock tried to land me in trouble with the UVF leadership and wanted to know if I had told people that I was going to kill him. Even though I was sitting in the headquarters of the UVF, I was not afraid to answer him. I told him that if he was telling the truth, that he knew nothing about my son's murder and that he was not involved in the cover-up to protect those who killed him, then he had nothing to be afraid of. However, I added: 'If you are lying, I will be coming for you and you know what that means.' His red olive face, the result of heavy drinking, turned a whiter shade of pale. He knew me and he knew that I didn't make empty threats.

The meeting ended and I left. On the way out a UVF man told me I had nothing to worry about going outside. I looked at him and said: 'Why should I worry about anybody here?'

Did they honestly believe I would be frightened to walk out on to the Shankill Road. I was not in the UVF and neither did I want to be, and as they would find out, I could look after myself against them. The UVF became more worried about me than I was about them. The fight for justice was starting to hot up and I was not going to rest until I uncovered the truth about my son's murder, the role Mark Haddock had played in his killing and the cover-up by the Special Branch. Threats from the UVF would intensify against me, but all my adult life the paramilitaries have foolishly tried to scare me without success. I know how my son died and I know he died fighting. He just didn't lie down. Neither the UVF nor the UDA will ever see me lie down to them either.

8.
The Hunt for Raymond's Killers

There is no greater pain in the world than losing a son or daughter. It is even worse when they are so cruelly taken away from you, beaten to a pulp, dumped in an isolated place and left to die alone with no one to help them. I have sat many nights on my own thinking of how Raymond must have suffered that night, how he must have cried out in pain as those evil bastards murdered him. The pain I felt when I lost my son is like nothing I had ever experienced before in my life. Losing a close relative is difficult, but when it is your own flesh and blood, a child you helped create and held in your arms in his first few minutes after he was born, it is simply unbearable. I felt so empty inside, almost numb at times. My heart has literally ached from the day the police came to my home and broke the news. I didn't just lose a son, I lost a very close friend, like the brother I never had.

But I was not going to allow my grief and my pain to deflect me from getting to the bottom of what I can only describe as the vicious and brutal murder of a lovely, kind young man who had his whole life ahead of him. Those who had killed him had made a fatal error of judgment. They thought they were untouchable, out of reach. But their downfall was to murder Raymond McCord Jnr and their crime was about to be exposed for all to see.

I started to dig into the murky world of the UVF looking for clues as to who was actually involved in my son's murder. I wanted to know why they had killed him. No one in north Belfast was saying very much, but I knew there were people in that community who would talk, some out of spite, others out of fear. Some people were helpful, but others I found out were lying to me. In no time at all different versions of the murder started to emerge, and I knew I had to check out each and every one to get to the truth.

One man contacted me and made arrangements for us to meet. I didn't realise at the time the danger I was in as the killers knew I was starting to ask a lot of questions and they couldn't risk having me uncover the truth. I was a dead man walking as far as they were concerned. They wanted me dead. During the meeting this individual told me some information he had. On the night Raymond was murdered there had been a fight at a Ballyduff shop and Raymond was involved in it. A woman who had witnessed the fight that night was too afraid to come forward and say anything. It had to be checked out and so along with a friend we arranged to see the woman. To protect her from any possible reprisal, we met her as she left work. The woman got into my car and she was clearly very nervous. She was not threatened and she was not forced. She got into the car of her own free will. After a few minutes my hopes were dashed when she informed me that there was no fight that night and that the story had been made up. I thanked the woman for her help and told her before she left my car that no one would know she had spoken to me. I haven't set eyes on her since.

Other stories surfaced from people who had their own

problems with the paramilitaries and suggested the names of the killers. One of the most interesting was from a man in Rathcoole. It was a Saturday afternoon and my mate Tommy picked me up in a taxi from my house in York Road and drove me to Bridge Street in the city centre. As I crossed the road, a man was waiting on the pavement who shook my hand and expressed his sympathy to me. I told Tommy to head on to the pub and I would meet up with him there. But Tommy, being Tommy, decided to wait just a few yards away. The man gave me the names of those he believed were the killers, all UDA men from Rathcoole, and said it was 100 per cent accurate. I thanked him, shook his hand and walked away. The story sounded plausible as those he named had a previous history with me. But over the next few days when I checked out the story, it turned out to be a pack of lies. What he didn't tell me was that he had given me the names of the UDA men who had beaten up his own son. He was trying to con me into doing his dirty work. He was a sad father to think that I wouldn't check out his story.

Like the police, my enquiries centred on the UVF and in particular its Mount Vernon gang. I had aunts and cousins living in Mount Vernon, but for all their talk at the funeral none of them lifted a finger to help my family in any way. In many ways I didn't need them, but they would have been helpful for information. It was left to the others in Mount Vernon to tell me anything they heard on the grapevine. Even some UVF men in Mount Vernon gave me information as they had no love for Haddock and his close associates. I was receiving similar information from different sources, including policemen, about who was involved. What I didn't know was why Haddock had young Raymond murdered. I also wasn't completely sure who owned the drugs that Raymond had been caught with in June 1997.

To find out about the drugs I had to go and meet some dangerous individuals — criminals, drug dealers, both loyalists and republicans — in their own backyards. At no time did I ever feel I was in any great danger although I know now that I took a lot of risks in meeting these people. But as far as I was concerned nothing was too big a risk for Raymond. All my sons would have done the same if I had been murdered. Drugs were starting to take a hold in Belfast, and loyalist paramilitaries, who had previously publicly denied being involved in the drug scene, were looking for a slice of the action as they could see there was big money to be made, even though they would be poisoning their own communities. Their mottos, 'For God and Ulster' (uvf) and *Quis Separabit* (uda), became 'How much dough can we make from blow?'

I also needed to know why Raymond had got himself involved in drugs. David Ervine, who represented the political wing of the uvf, the Progressive Unionist Party (pup), once branded my son a drug dealer on bbc Radio Ulster. The station later had to apologise for what he said, but Ervine never did, even though he said he would consider it. Unlike some of Ervine's friends and drinking buddies among the loyalist paramilitaries, my son wasn't a drug dealer. Jim 'Jonty' Johnston, the murdered brigadier of the Red Hand Commando terror group in north Down, made a fortune from drug dealing. His activities were exposed by the Assets Recovery Agency who stripped him of his home and cash which it said was derived from the proceeds of drug dealing and money laundering. This is the same Jimmy Johnston who paraded Ervine around Belfast in his 4 x 4 jeep after he was first elected to Belfast City Hall as a pup councillor, and the same Jimmy Johnston who gave Ervine money towards his suits and his constituency office in east Belfast. People in glass houses shouldn't throw stones. The only reason why my son got involved in drugs was because he had no money and no job and he foolishly believed in the words of sinister people that it was an easy way to make money with little risk involved.

Throughout the course of my enquiries, criminal elements in Belfast told me that the drugs belonged to Mark Haddock. Some members of the security forces also confirmed to me that the drugs did indeed belong to Haddock. As Haddock was in jail, there was no way I could confront him about the drugs and I decided to speak to his brigadier, Rab Warnock, another convicted UVF man and a coward who hid behind the organisation's name. Just after Raymond's murder I spoke to Warnock at his home and also at the Monkstown Social Club which the UVF controlled. His attitude was that he wanted to help me get the killers. When I asked him about the drugs, all he would say was that he didn't know who owned them, or maybe he was too afraid to tell me. I also met him one day by arrangement in York Road, a loyalist stronghold. He was accompanied by another UVF member, a convicted killer from Mount Vernon. I invited Warnock to get into my car, which he did quite freely. As the other guy was about to get into the back seat, I told him to wait on the footpath. It wasn't a request and he stood outside. I told Warnock who owned the drugs. I said that I had been reliably informed from a number of sources, including the police, that the drugs belonged to Haddock, his CO in Mount Vernon. Warnock's jaw dropped and he said: 'I'm gutted.' It was a performance worthy of any actor and at the time I believed him. But I found out later that he was lying. My first thought after that meeting was that he would tell the UVF leadership on the Shankill Road and they would deal with Haddock and the killers. However, Warnock had no intention of dropping Haddock in trouble with the leadership. There was money to be made from drugs and Warnock was getting his cut of the profits. Why would he kill the goose that was laying him the golden eggs? Even when I met a senior UVF man, Mr V, from the Cregagh estate in east Belfast and told him who owned the drugs, all he could say was, 'Where's the proof?'

I needed to get proof. It was going to be difficult but not impossible. Other individuals in Belfast knew about the drugs but were too frightened to say anything about Haddock. They all knew he was a killer. But then one day I struck lucky and found out that somebody had been in Mount Vernon with Raymond when he was talking to Haddock about the drugs. This was the positive break-through I needed. I phoned the UVF man from the Cregagh estate and we arranged to meet in my favourite pub, the Monico. We met on a Saturday afternoon when the bar was very busy. The UVF man, Mr V, asked me what proof I had and I told him that a man now living in England was prepared to come over to Belfast and tell the UVF about Haddock and his involvement in drugs. Mr V asked me the name of my source, but I refused to give it to him as I was concerned as to what might happen to him if his name was divulged. I then suggested to Mr V that I would arrange for my source to ring the Monico at a certain time so that he could ask him some questions. Mr V wanted to see the man in person and I suggested that I could bring him over from England and meet him in a place that I would pick and where he would be under my protection. Mr V knew what I meant by that. Even though this man was prepared to come back to Belfast and spill the beans to the head of the UVF's internal security, Mr V lost all interest in the matter. Years later I found out that Mr V was also an informer and there was no way he was going to his UVF boss about another informer selling drugs. I was back to square one again.

Months went by and the RUC had still made no progress in their murder investigation. Unknown to our family, Haddock had still not been questioned even though he was in jail and was the prime suspect for ordering Raymond's murder. It took fourteen weeks, over three months, before the RUC questioned him. By this time some people connected with the loyalist paramilitaries warned me to be extra careful as Haddock and his thugs were not too happy about me shining a light into the dark corners of their underworld. I was told that Haddock, his associates and his police handlers were starting to get worried. To me, that could only mean one thing, that my hunt for the killers was on the right road. One way of keeping the spotlight on Raymond's murder and trying to rattle the killers was through the media. It had become the norm in Northern Ireland that when someone was murdered, it was front page news with policemen and politicians condemning those responsible.

But the only ones talking about the killing were the victim's family. I never dreamt that I would have to keep running to the media, but the more I investigated my son's murder, the more murky and sinister it became. The police and politicians don't like the media hounding them and that was slowly starting to happen in this case. When I first started telling the media and the general public about Haddock and his unit, my words were being dismissed as the ranting of a father still in mourning. Unfortunately, for a long time that was how I was widely perceived. But why would I want to lie about who murdered my son? I had nothing to gain from peddling lies and I certainly didn't want to misinform the general public.

Some in the media were having second thoughts about

what I had to say. But very few politicians were willing to push my case at the outset. However, Nigel Dodds of the Democratic Unionist Party (DUP) did accompany me to a meeting with the then RUC Chief Constable Ronnie Flanagan, and Ian Paisley Jnr, the son of the DUP leader, Rev. Ian Paisley, attended a meeting with myself and an assistant chief constable. After those meetings I heard nothing more from the DUP politicians and I often wondered was this simply a cosmetic exercise, just going through the motions for my sake.

The UVF believed that after a while I would get fed up making my own enquiries and that I would go away. It showed how little they knew about me, Vivienne and our sons. At no time did any of us give up the hunt for Raymond's killers. At this stage we were only looking for the killers, not the corrupt RUC officers who were covering up their tracks. Not a day or a week went by that I didn't meet or receive a phone call from someone which provided information that would form another part of the jigsaw. It showed in some way that they cared and it was the fuel that kept me going.

On one occasion I met a policeman and his wife in the dimly lit docks area of Belfast. Their car pulled into a street and parked in front of mine. The policeman was in plain clothes. I recognised his wife from a few days earlier when I bumped into them in Belfast city centre while they were out shopping. He said he had heard I was talking about him and Haddock. I said that was true. He said he would ring me later to arrange a meeting. What I didn't know then was that the security forces had tapped my phone and were listening to my calls. As I sat in the back of the policeman's car, another car drove past with a man and woman on board. I don't believe it was a coincidence. I found it strange that any man would take his wife or girlfriend for a drive in that area of Belfast so late at night. My suspicions were further aroused when they paid us a little more attention than I would have expected from an ordinary couple. We had either been followed or the security forces knew about the meeting from the telephone intercept. It appeared that the security forces were worried about our meeting. The policeman was trying to find out how much I knew. When I told him the names of the UVF men who were informers and who were also involved in serious crime, he looked quite taken aback. He was careful about what he said and I wondered if he was worried about something concerning Haddock. I didn't tell him everything I knew, just enough to make him sit up and take notice. The meeting ended after about twenty minutes and I drove away in my car. I was never as glad to leave a place as it was such an isolated part of Belfast docks.

The policeman contacted me the following day and told me he and his wife were stunned about what I had told them, particularly about Haddock, informants and corrupt policemen. He said the information I had could only have come from the police. I said there were good officers in the RUC who wanted justice and wanted to help me. The policeman confirmed that Haddock was a Special Branch informer and that he had ordered Raymond's murder. When I named the others involved in his killing, he didn't disagree, indicating that the information was genuine and correct.

But it wasn't all good news. The murder investigation appeared to be lost in no man's land and those in charge would not admit to me that Haddock was a Special Branch informer. If only they had shown real courage like other more honourable policemen, then Raymond's killers along with Haddock would have been through the courts long ago. Even though the detectives knew Haddock was a 'protected species' within the Special Branch, they chose to stay quiet. I believe they should either have gone after Haddock and his associates in a determined way or resigned. Disgracefully, as far as I am concerned, they chose to stay silent and collected their wages every month. I don't believe any man or woman joins the police force to turn a blind eye to murder, drug dealing, kneecapping, extortion or intimidation. Hopefully they make every effort to behave as honourable, decent men and carry out their duties to the best of their ability. But somehow I doubt it. I wonder how many more people have died because of collusion and police officers staying silent.

As time passed, more and more information was coming my way from people who wanted to help. I found it hard to accept how a working-class welder from north Belfast could accumulate so much information, whereas the RUC couldn't or wouldn't with all the informants they had operating at the heart of the UVF. On several occasions I met very senior police officers and each time the same old story was trotted out. They were making enquiries into this or that and they would keep me informed about developments. We knew who had murdered Raymond and who had ordered his murder, so my family couldn't understand what further enquiries the RUC, and later the Police Service of Northern Ireland (PSNI), had yet to make. I think they were stalling for time for some reason, but I was later told in private conversations with police officers that any investigation they were involved in, which were directly related to the activities of Mark Haddock, whether it was for murder or any other serious terrorist crime, always hit a brick wall. It was their coded way of telling me that Haddock was out of bounds, off limits, a protected species, a top Special Branch informant inside Mount Vernon UVF.

There were times when I was so deeply frustrated, but I

was never going to give up. I too would sometimes hit a brick wall, but somehow I found the strength, spurred on probably by my son, to find another way around the obstacle. It was not in me to give up. I had come too far now to stop. It was going to be a matter of slowly chipping away at this brick wall until it would collapse in a pile of rubble. I didn't care how long this took. I was in this for the long haul.

I would lie in bed at night unable to sleep with so many thoughts racing through my head. One of the things that was troubling me was how the UVF lured Raymond to his death. I knew my son and I know he would not have gone voluntarily to his death. There had to be an explanation as to how they were able to convince him to go with them. When I eventually found out what happened, I was stunned. Raymond received a phone call from the Maze Prison from his mate Darren Moore, who wanted to see him. Raymond went to see him on Saturday, 8 November 1997, the last day he was seen alive. It was the day he was taken by Bonzo Bond in a car driven by Stephen Logue. I have since discovered that Moore told my son that the UVF were going to shoot him in the leg, give him a flesh wound, over the drugs. Following that meeting in the jail, the three drove back to north Belfast. Raymond went home and changed out of a pair of good trousers into an old pair for the kneecapping. But the story Moore told him was a lie. He had Judased my son and helped send him to his death. This was how he repaid a good friend who looked after him when he was homeless.

The more I uncovered about my son's murder, the more shocked I became about betrayal, collusion and cover-up. My search for the truth was starting to shatter the nerves of senior UVF people who knew the more I probed, the more I would find. It was like peeling an onion: as each layer was removed, I discovered more dark secrets.

In smoke-filled UVF clubs in north Belfast a plan was being devised to kill me. Those who didn't agree with this were keeping me quietly informed so that I could vary my movements and redouble my personal security. I was obviously getting under the skin of senior UVF figures and causing them serious damage. Their political mouthpiece David Ervine was also rattled and couldn't deal with the media over my son. He was once quoted in the press as saying: 'Raymond McCord must be the most written about father in Europe.' But what else did this convicted UVF bomber want me to do, lie down and be trampled over by the scum who murdered young Raymond, the same scum who were members of a paramilitary organisation he had belonged to all his life? My campaign for justice was something completely new to the UVF and the PUP — a Protestant, unionist father in their community fighting back against a crowd of UVF scumbags who were doing the police's dirty work.

UVF threats on my life were not having the desired effect. I was refusing to go away, to bend the knee to them. I was told that there was a real fear inside the highest ranks of the UVF that our hunt for Raymond's killers was going to unmask more informants, not just among the ordinary rank-and-file 'foot soldiers', but also at the most senior levels of the terrorist group. I was also told that the UVF leadership were genuinely afraid of me and of what other secrets I would uncover about their organisation. Instead of doing the decent, honourable thing and handing my son's killers over to the RUC/PSNI, they assisted the cover-up in the hope that it would come to nothing.

They tried intimidation. One night graffiti appeared all over the Newtownabbey area, on main roads and entrances to housing estates. It read: 'Which son next daddy Raymond?

Gareth or Glenn? Your choice.' As Gareth and I were trying to remove one from the entrance to the estate where Vivienne lived so she would not see it, the police arrived to give us more bad news. The UVF had stooped to a new level of depravity and deployed a new tactic to try and shut me up. Someone used the cover of darkness to go into Carnmoney Cemetery one night and smashed Raymond's headstone. Even in death they wouldn't let him rest in peace. It was a concerted and orchestrated campaign by south east Antrim UVF to frustrate my pursuit of justice. It was the same UVF from whom David Ervine had said my family and I had nothing to fear, that we were not in any danger. When we arrived at the cemetery and saw the damage, I felt angry and disgusted. The organisation that did this celebrated the Battle of the Somme, the same organisation which claimed to exist to protect the unionist community. The UVF had, in my eyes, stooped to a new low against my family. No one in the UVF could explain to me how the desecration of young Raymond's grave had helped the UVF in their battle against the IRA. When people threaten my sons, I repay them with a visit. It was no different on this occasion. I knew that the UVF leadership of south east Antrim UVF drank in the Monkstown Social Club and this was the place to confront them.

When I walked into the club, everyone suddenly stopped talking. Complete silence. There was no sign of any of the leadership, so I went to the brigadier Rab Warnock's home. Again no luck, but the neighbours and the people at the club would tell him that I was determined to speak to him. I drove to Monkstown several times to Warnock's home looking for him. People probably thought I was reckless, but I had lost one son and I wasn't going to lose another. Soon word filtered through to Warnock from unknown quarters that if the UVF went near Gareth or Glenn, then every member of his family and his relatives would be targeted. The message was passed down to rank and file UVF men under his command, and my sons were left alone. I discovered that if you confront thugs at their front door, they soon back down. During the course of the police investigation, the names of those who had smashed Raymond's headstone came to light, but no one was ever arrested. That didn't surprise me or my family in the least. We didn't let that affect our campaign.

Each week the media carried stories about the activities of the Mount Vernon UVF. The *Sunday World* newspaper was behind us every step of the way in our campaign. With the pressure mounting through the *Sunday World*, other newspapers and television, the UVF dispatched another team on a second 'military operation' and smashed my son's headstone again. To add insult to injury, these brave UVF men also smashed a marble memorial at the grave which was a personal tribute from Gareth and Glenn. The men who died at the Battle of the Somme would have been just as disgusted as we were at how the modern day UVF were behaving. I saw little point in contacting my local MLA, the PUP's Billy Hutchinson, whose office was just around the corner from my house, about this latest act of wanton destruction. Hutchinson, had served a life sentence for the double UVF murder of two Catholics in the 1970s. After the first attack on the headstone I contacted his office, but he refused to talk to me over the phone. His secretary informed me that he wouldn't talk to me as I had already spoken to the press. I had nothing but contempt for him. As far as I was concerned, he was just another loyalist coward. It was clear to me that the PUP wanted to smother my protests about the attack on Raymond's headstone and about the graffiti threats to my two other sons. As far as I could see the PUP were operating double standards. It was all right for them to appear on television, but the victims were to have no voice and could not speak out. But this was not Nazi Germany; this was Northern Ireland in the 1990s, and my family was not going to be silenced by bully boy tactics.

On the morning of the second attack on the headstone, Glenn and I went to the grave. I just cried my heart out at the scene of devastation. How could anyone do this and what sort of people are they, I asked myself. Members of the Catholic community from the nearby village of Whiteabbey came over to express their sympathy and disgust. They lifted bits of the headstone up off the grass and attempted to put it together again. I will not forget their act of kindness. But their efforts at repairing it were in vain and a new headstone and a new memorial from Gareth and Glenn were needed.

I left the graveyard that morning in a distressed state, trying not to let Glenn see me cry, and headed down to the local RUC station where I spoke to a woman detective sergeant. I was still very angry. She informed me that enquiries would be made, but other than that there was very little they could do as there were no witnesses. I found her attitude disgraceful. I asked her to question the UVF's area brigadier Rab Warnock, because nothing would happen unless he gave it the green light. She said that would be impossible as they had no proof that he was involved. But I knew that people had been arrested before with no proof and their front doors smashed in without any proof either. It appeared to me that the RUC were using this as a lame duck excuse not to investigate the desecration of my son's headstone. But something had to be done and I told her that I personally would go to Warnock's door and speak to him about it myself. She asked me what I would do if he admitted it. I said I would arrest him, I would make a citizen's arrest. She tried to dissuade me from going, saying Warnock might have men at his house. I replied 'Good' and left the police station to take Glenn home to collect his kit as he was playing a football match. After dropping Glenn off at the football ground I went back home and broke down in my living room. I felt like screaming, but I knew I could not let the UVF scum who had done this beat me. I pulled myself together and was wiping the tears away from my eyes when my front door bell rang. I opened the door and there were two uniformed police officers standing there. I thought they had come to tell me they had some information about the attack on the headstone. One of the officers, who could see I was still distressed, told me that they had come to arrest me. I thought I was hearing things. It was just hours after finding Raymond's headstone smashed by the UVF, and the RUC wanted to arrest me. The officer asked me if I had assaulted or threatened anyone. I said I was just back into my house after dropping Glenn off at a football match, and I asked him if he knew about the attack on the headstone and that that was why I was upset. He asked me again if I had been anywhere else, and I said no. He then asked me if he could use my phone. Over the phone he told whoever he was talking to that I had not left the house. But it made no difference. The person at the other end told him I was to be arrested. No reason was given and I was put in the back of a police car and driven to the Antrim Road Police Station, even though there was an RUC station just around the corner from me. At the police station I was fingerprinted, my trousers belt was removed and I was put in a cell. I was asked if I had any medical problems. When I told them I took tablets for back pain, I was later examined by a police doctor. I told the doctor about my back pain and that I was upset over the smashing of my son's headstone. It made no difference and I was passed fit for interview. As I waited in my cell, I wondered what the hell was going on. I was subsequently taken by a uniformed police officer to an interview room. A male detective walked in along with the female detective sergeant from Whiteabbey Police Station I had spoken to earlier. They questioned me, without a solicitor being present, about Rab Warnock and they asked me what I was going to do. She alleged that I had told her I was going to get a gun and shoot Warnock. It was entirely untrue. Who in their right mind would say something like that to a police officer in a police station? During my interview, which was recorded, I totally refuted her allegations. The male detective told me I would be going to Maghaberry Prison, but he was only trying to frighten me and it wasn't working. I knew that what the police woman was saying was untrue and they could not prove her allegations. The thrust of the interview was that they didn't want me going anywhere near Warnock's home and they had placed two undercover cars near his house just in case I paid him a visit. Why were the police so keen to protect Warnock, I wondered. I told them I wanted to be released as I had to collect my son Glenn from his football match. The male CID officer just laughed at me. I thought it would be nice to spend just five minutes up a dark alley with him where I could teach him some manners and see how much he laughed then.

No one would tell me if I was to be released or charged, but I knew my rights and I demanded to make a phone call. I phoned my friend Tommy, who said that if I was charged he would post bail for me. I was brought back into the interview room and the male detective informed me that I was being released on condition that I stayed out of the Monkstown estate. I thought they were going overboard to protect Warnock, but I agreed. I was released without charge. During the whole interview not once did either express any sympathy or concern about the smashing of Raymond's headstone or the distress and upset it was causing my family. All they cared about was protecting Warnock from me and keeping me out of Monkstown. I hadn't the slightest intention of staying out of Monkstown and I went looking for Warnock again but I couldn't find him. I later learned that he had brought down a large team of men from Mount Vernon to his club to protect him in case I showed up. Later that day I rang him while he was in the club. He invited me down and told me about the team he had with him. I told him I would have a yarn with him some night when he was walking home from the club or I might even call down some night to his house unannounced. Strangely, a short time after this, an arsonist torched his new car. For some peculiar reason the RUC thought I had burned his car, but I told them that that would have been against the law!

Over the years the RUC/PSNI arrested me at my house, stopped my car on several occasions to search it, and arrested me at gunpoint in a graveyard while I was talking to another man. It was pure intimidation and harassment by the security agencies who were trying to stop me from getting at the truth. Every time they arrested me it gave me great heart because someone in the UVF was getting worried that I was creeping ever closer to the truth. With the help of the media over the past ten years, my family and I have achieved our goal of exposing collusion and killers getting away with murder. But it wasn't always the case, and at the outset I don't think the media realised there was something rotten at the heart of the criminal justice system in Northern Ireland. And nobody, not even I, could have foreseen just how rotten it had become.

One night I received a phone call to my home from a

much-respected journalist. He wanted to meet me the following day as he was not prepared to talk over the phone. A safe meeting place was arranged and as we sat talking over a cup of tea, he informed me of a contact of his in London who was aware of dirty deeds going on in Northern Ireland. He never told me who his source was, but I believed the contact was either a member of the British Labour Party or involved in British military defence. The message conveyed to me was very simple: 'Tell Raymond McCord to keep going and it will come out. Tell him he is causing real ructions in London among certain people and they are getting very worried.' My campaign for justice was striking right at the heart of the government in London. It proved to me that with the help of the media in keeping the spotlight on young Raymond's case, we were unsettling people and shaking them to the foundations of their cosy existence. Certain people had something to worry about, something they didn't want brought into the public arena.

In seeking justice for my son, I told the media about the UVF's involvement in drug dealing, in particular Mount Vernon and Mark Haddock. As expected, the UVF didn't like these stories and it reacted in the way I had come to expect. On one occasion the police stopped a car going into Mount Vernon with £1 million worth of drugs on board. The PUP said that if the drugs belonged to the UVF, then they would have to consider their position. Billy Hutchinson told the media that the UVF would conduct an inquiry. That inquiry has lasted longer than the Bloody Sunday inquiry and no one has ever heard a result. The fact was I was telling the truth and the UVF couldn't handle that. Their leadership may have been opposed to drugs, but people it put in charge of certain areas were knee deep in drug dealing and they did nothing to stop them. Instead they preferred to kill Protestants on the streets of Belfast and beyond, and they were also trying to kill me and silence me once and for all.

I lived throughout this period under constant threat. I made a vow very early on in my campaign that every time the RUC/PSNI called at my home with an official warning that the UVF were planning an attack on me, I would visit the homes of UVF men either by sitting outside in my car or knocking on their front doors. My attitude was that if they sent people looking for me, I would come looking for them. They were brave men in a crowd, but on their own they were frightened wee boys. Fear can be a terrible thing when you are on your own and you don't have an organisation to protect you. UVF threats and intimidation came in many forms — smashing my son's headstone, painting graffiti and hatching plots to commit murder. They even sent a sympathy card to my 81-year-old mother on the death of her son, me. But it would take a lot to frighten my mother Kathleen because she is as brave as they come. When she received the card she rang me. Her concern was not what the UVF would do to me, but what I would do to them. She knew only too well that I would not succumb to threats or intimidation.

In another attempt to muzzle me, they placed a hoax bomb outside the home of a personal friend who has stood by me through thick and thin. John Niblock was a 76-year-old pensioner who drank with me regularly. Because of his association with me the UVF tried to intimidate him by leaving the device at his front door. But it did not drive a wedge between us or end our friendship. In fact it strengthened our friendship and I will never forget John's fortitude in defying the UVF and continuing to socialise with me. John was like my mate Tommy Benson, who also stuck by me.

I knew the UVF were worried and I would leave no stone

unturned to get to the heart of my son's murder. I had to check that what I found out was correct. In doing so I had to meet some very unsavoury people to corroborate the allegations. I make no apologies for that. I met dangerous and ruthless drug dealers on their own turf to find out what they had heard; I met UVF and UDA men privately who were trying their best to get information for me. Even republicans contacted me to let me know what they had heard; and RUC men broke rank to provide me with information as well as journalists who had contacts in both the security forces and the paramilitaries. I was literally prepared to meet anyone, any time, any place, anywhere. At great personal risk to myself, I went into pubs and clubs where I normally would not have ventured, sat at a table in the corner and waited to meet a contact. I received some strange looks and at times I was very nervous, but I knew I had to do it. I could almost touch and taste the truth, I was getting that close. But still I had to be absolutely certain about the killers' identities.

The most satisfying part of this journey towards truth and justice was that the killers knew I was getting ever closer to them. Everyone in Mount Vernon knew who killed Raymond and who had ordered it, but they were too frightened to speak. But the day will come when these people will summon the courage to stand up to the thugs. If I could find the courage to face them down, then so can they. A coward hates to be confronted. My courage was born out of a promise to my murdered son and my battle for him was supported by a close group of friends. My two sons are my best friends along with close pals Frank, Tommy, John, Johnny, Seamus, Jackie, Roy, Kenny and Simpy. Some of these I have known all my life, while others I only met since young Raymond was murdered. These men whom I trusted with my life were constantly watching my back, warning me of hidden dangers lurking around the next corner. How many UVF men could say they have even one real friend they could trust with their life? From what I have discovered, not very many in an organisation riddled with informers. My close circle of friends spurred me on, along with the help of the general public. They were an inspiration as I hunted for Raymond's killers. Many would stop me in the street and shake my hand, telling me not to give up; others I met while on holiday wished me well and gave me words of advice and encouragement. Their kindness and warmth lifted my heart at times when I was at a low point in my life. They often asked me if I thought my son's killers would get what they deserved. I always answered yes, because I believe what goes around, comes around. But I never thought, within the space of ten years from my son's murder, that Mount Vernon UVF would be finished. Then again, they had never killed a McCord before and they had never killed a Protestant from a family who wouldn't rest until his killers were exposed.

9.
Mount Vernon UVF Unmasked

Mount Vernon is a small housing estate situated in the loyalist Shore Road area of north Belfast. At the entrance to the estate are two large, multi-storey blocks of flats housing several hundred people. The most striking and eye-catching part of the estate from the road is a large mural depicting masked UVF gunmen emblazoned with the slogan, 'Ready for Peace, Prepared for War.' Unfortunately for the Protestant community in north Belfast and beyond, the UVF unit in Mount Vernon had no interest in peace. They only cared about murder and making large sums of money from drug dealing, extortion, loan sharking, money laundering and prostitution. But Mount Vernon UVF didn't do this alone. The organisation's leadership willingly turned a blind eye to the activities of its leader Mark Haddock and his tout-ridden unit who ruled the estate through fear and with an iron fist gripping either a baseball bat or a gun.

The RUC/PSNI should have been the authority in Mount Vernon as it was seen in the eyes of ordinary, working-class people as the force of law and order. However, the reality of the situation was somewhat different. A senior UVF man,

Mark Haddock, who was also a leading RUC/PSNI Special Branch informant, ran the estate like a feudal lord ran his fiefdom. With the police turning a blind eye to his terrorist and criminal activities, Haddock became more powerful and he was able to spread fear way beyond the boundary of Mount Vernon. Even when I had meetings with the UVF leadership on the Shankill Road I never left their company believing they would truly deal with Haddock. At its most basic, he was a killer who made huge pots of money for the UVF through drug dealing and extortion and it seemed the leadership were more interested in lining their own pockets than removing a scourge from the community. Even the UVF's political wing paid little heed to Haddock's activities. The local PUP MLA, Billy Hutchinson, claimed he had his 'ear to the ground' and would know what was happening in the area. Yet he didn't seem to know about the serious drug-dealing activities of Haddock and his mob. I can only think that the ear Billy Hutchinson had to the ground must have been a deaf ear, or perhaps he was one of the very few among many thousands who didn't know Haddock was a drug dealer.

Over the years Mount Vernon had earned itself a bad name and on occasions several Catholics were shot dead in the estate just because they were Catholics in the wrong place at the wrong time. But the killers did not get away with it and the RUC arrested several UVF men from Mount Vernon who were later convicted and sentenced to life in prison. Thankfully, the families of those murdered Catholics received some justice. I still have relatives living in Mount Vernon, cousins, aunts and uncles, where most of the men are members of the UVF. In the 1970s the IRA went to the home of one of my uncles and tried to kill him and other members of his family. However, though my uncle was shot, he fortunately survived the attempt on his life. It was as a result of my extended family's connections that people had a preconception that I must have been in some way sympathetic to the UVF, but this was never the case. Several times in the late 1970s I fought with some of the UVF men from Mount Vernon and was able to walk away. Most of the hard men of Belfast did not belong to any paramilitary group because they didn't want to join up. But Mount Vernon was not a place I would have often ventured into, as there was really no need to. On a few occasions I was in my uncle's house and my Aunt Barbara always made me feel welcome. She had had a hard life what with having to visit the jail for many years where her sons had been locked up for various UVF activities. It seemed she spent more time on jail visits than she did in her own home. However, another aunt, Annie, didn't have those problems. Annie was a homely person too and she always treated me kindly when I visited her. Her son Billy is one of life's gentlemen and he and his wife Margaret are two of the few McCords who never shunned me out of fear of the UVF.

Mount Vernon was made up mostly of families who had previously lived in York Street and the narrow streets that ran from it. All my relatives came from the back streets off York Street. In the summer of 2000 my Aunt Annie died and her family felt her loss deeply, none more so than her son Billy, who like myself never got involved with the paramilitaries. With a death threat hanging over my head from Mount Vernon UVF, most people assumed that I would not be able to attend her funeral for fear of being shot. But I decided to give the UVF a surprise and show Mark Haddock and his outfit that I had no fear of them by attending Aunt Annie's funeral. My son Glenn was with me.

On that day the vast majority of the people in Mount

Vernon saw the true side of Haddock & Co. It didn't take long for the UVF jungle drums to start beating and word soon spread that I was at the funeral. A UVF mob gathered down the street from my aunt's house and bravely they jeered and waved at me. These are the same people who don't allow the dead to rest in peace. I remember them shouting from a distance, 'Daddy Raymond', but not one of them was brave enough to approach me. They hurled all their abuse at me from a safe distance. These were the men who would fight for Ulster. As we were about to walk behind the hearse, an elderly lady called me over. One of her sons was in the UVF, but that didn't stop the woman shaking my hand in defiance of the rabble further down the street. She wished me good luck and said the ordinary people of Mount Vernon were glad to see me. After the funeral I left the estate and have only returned around a dozen times since, hoping to see certain individuals walking about so that I could deal with them in my own way over young Raymond's murder. That day in Mount Vernon showed the good people of the estate what the local UVF were like, but it also showed Mount Vernon UVF that not everyone feared them. That message was slowly but surely being driven home to them, and they didn't like it.

As time passed, and with the help of the newspapers, in particular the *Sunday World*, the people of Mount Vernon came to know how many murders had been carried out under Mark Haddock's instructions and why there were so few prosecutions. Everyone knew that Haddock and his cronies were killers. Many suspected that he was a police tout, but no one dared say it. Through fear and collusion with the Special Branch, Haddock didn't even need to wear a mask or balaclava when committing serious crimes. His handlers ensured that he was protected from the law to keep him in place.

There was the occasion in 1992 when Haddock tried to kill

an innocent Catholic taxi driver. The murder bid failed when the gun jammed and the cabbie grappled with Haddock. The intended victim was later able to give the police a description of his attacker from a photo-fit montage, which resembled Haddock, as the would-be gunman was so cocky he didn't bother to wear a mask. Haddock fled the scene, but he had dropped the gun during the struggle, which had the potential to provide forensic evidence. However, despite having the intended murder weapon, the photo-fit and a description of tattoos on his arms, Haddock was never arrested. Absolutely no action was taken against him, even though he was the prime suspect in the eyes of investigating CID detectives. Unfortunately for the intended victim, the same UVF unit tried to kill him five years later, but again they were unsuccessful. Again Haddock was not arrested, even though he was the prime suspect, as he was known to have been in the area at the time.

Unknown to me, incidents such as these became the norm due to his relationship with the Special Branch. A policy appeared to have been adopted by the Special Branch that informants were of no use in jail even if they were killing people. To me, that is collusion. I am sure there are many families today who would like some retribution for losing a loved one and for the police to momentarily turn a blind eye to the sort of street justice that the paramilitary killers deserve. But due to a policy developed by senior RUC men, the taking of human life meant very little to these men. There was a bigger picture involved and human beings were being sacrificed as a consequence. Life had become cheap. Think of the countless people who would be alive today including my son if the RUC had done its job back in 1992 and arrested, charged and convicted Haddock for the attempted murder of the taxi driver.

Over the years since young Raymond's murder I have met many police officers and asked them why they were doing nothing to bring Haddock and his gang to book for serious terrorist crimes, which it appeared to me were being carried out quite openly. The usual answer was, they needed proof or they needed to catch them at the scene. But they already had proof. They simply failed to act on it. As regards catching them at the scene, I know that the police watched over a UVF drug den just to protect a member of the organisation who was a fully paid-up police agent, Willie Glendinning.

Glendinning was selling cannabis and Ecstasy tablets from his house in the Rathcoole estate. His house being adjacent to a school, the kids would call each day for their drugs. This was happening during daylight hours in the middle of a housing estate. It was like the kids were queuing up for ice cream or sweets, but they were actually buying drugs from a UVF member who was also a police informant. It was a disgrace. Some residents in Rathcoole contacted me about the drug house and I arranged to meet the police at Whiteabbey Police Station. Two CID officers, an inspector and a sergeant, met me. When I explained that drugs were being sold from the house to schoolchildren, the sergeant told the inspector they had an ongoing operation in the area. What he really meant was the police were making sure the dealer was protected. The neighbours knew what was going on and so did the kids and many others in Rathcoole, but the police took no action. Glendinning's house was never searched or raided. I subsequently learned that he was the getaway driver the night Haddock shot dead Sharon McKenna in 1993. It came as no surprise when in early 2007 the PSNI moved Glendinning and his family out of Northern Ireland as the UVF had discovered he was a long-standing Special Branch informant. It was more evidence of collusion involving the State and a terrorist who was also a drug dealer.

The police's 'bigger picture' policy included Mark Haddock selling drugs out of a band hall close to the edge of the estate on the main Shore Road into Belfast city centre. Every Saturday night the hall would be packed with young people looking to buy drugs. It had no licence to sell drink, yet on either side of the hall just a few hundred yards apart were two police stations. For reasons known only to the police, the hall was allowed to stay open until five o'clock in the morning. Revellers came and went at all hours of the night and day, yet the police ignored them. Profits from the sale of drink and drugs lined the pockets of the UVF and Haddock. It was just a stone's throw from local PUP MLA Billy Hutchinson's office, yet he never once asked for it to be closed down. During the UVF feud with Johnny Adair's UDA on the Shankill Road, I watched Hutchinson on the television news talking about a drug house in the Lower Shankill estate which Adair controlled, yet he never condemned Haddock. As far as I am concerned, you do not pick and choose whom you condemn. It is either a crime or it is not; it is as simple as that. Why were the police tolerating an illegal shebeen which sold alcohol and drugs? The answer is, I believe, because the Special Branch had ruled it out of bounds to uniformed police and the CID as they had an informant at work inside.

One Saturday night I sat in my car just thirty yards from the shebeen watching people go inside. I was staggered on seeing one of my relatives opening the door to let people in. You can pick your friends but you can't pick your family, I thought. I left for a while but went back to the shebeen in the early hours of the morning in the hope of seeing Haddock and a few of his mates walking home. I was full of good intentions. As I sat there waiting for them, a police Land

Rover drove past and stopped some fifty yards from me. One of the officers got out and looked back towards my car. I don't know if he recognised me or not, but I thought it would be wise to drive off as there was always another day. It was disappointing. I was hoping that might be the night I could have had a little chat with Haddock and his thugs.

As a result of police inaction over the shebeen and the selling of drugs, I had a meeting with senior police officers, including two assistant chief constables. Privately, a police officer told me to ignore what was happening in the band hall because when some UVF men were stoned out of their heads on drugs, their tongues loosened and informants could pick up information from them for the police. Ah, the bigger picture! I thought. But surely the police and the UVF must have known other activities were going on inside the hall. Young men and girls, some just 13 years of age, were frequent visitors. Mount Vernon UVF members found it an easy way to have young girls flocking around them. First they got the girls hooked on free drugs, mainly with Ecstasy tablets. After a while the girls, who were still at school, expected more free drugs. But the senior UVF men in the hall had other ideas. Their attitude was that if the girls wanted more 'E' tabs, then in return they wanted free sex. A situation had developed where senior UVF men were having underage sex with teenage girls, yet the police drove past at night and allowed the band hall to stay open.

UVF men, who claimed to be defending Ulster from republicans, had resorted to giving young girls drugs for illicit sex. Their activities would shame and disgust the men who fought at the Battle of the Somme, the genuine UVF, not the pretenders. The most galling aspect of the band hall's illegal activities was that Special Branch informants were supplying the drugs. I have often wondered if the police had the band hall bugged. If they did, then they must have known exactly what was happening regarding drug dealing and underage sex with schoolgirls. The Special Branch controlled Mount Vernon UVF, so I find it hard to believe they didn't know what was going on. It seems to me they turned a blind eye because the hall was part of the 'bigger picture'. The local community was constantly whispering about what was happening in the band hall at the weekends, but again people were afraid to speak out openly about it. They couldn't turn to the police because they didn't know who to trust. Every so often there would be a murder, a kneecapping or a punishment beating in north Belfast, yet no names were ever mentioned and certainly no mention of Mount Vernon UVF. It reminded me of the film *Serpico*, which was about an American policeman who discovered how corrupt the police were in his area. But this wasn't America; this was Belfast and nobody would have thought the police would collude with loyalist paramilitaries in the murder, attempted murder or beatings of Protestants.

At this time some sections of the Northern Ireland media would not name Haddock and his associates. But some newspapers, including the *Sunday World*, came close to unmasking him. I knew deep down that that would change eventually. Until they were finally exposed, I kept a steady stream of stories appearing in the newspapers about Mount Vernon UVF and their criminal associates. These stories were not a figment of my imagination; they were true. Eventually Haddock would overstep the mark and make a major mistake which even the Special Branch would find difficult to cover up.

In December 2002 Trevor Gowdy, a security doorman and a former Territorial Army boxing champion from Ballyclare, Co. Antrim, would end Haddock's reign of terror. I have never met Trevor, but from what I have been told he was a hard man who, like me, didn't need to use baseball bats when dealing with paramilitaries during his work as a bouncer. He was the sort of person I would have wanted on my side if I was in a tight spot and the odds were stacked against me. Gowdy had a run-in one night with a few of Haddock's associates outside a public house in Ballyclare. He was able to handle the situation and Haddock's men came off second best and sent packing with their tails between their legs. I would not have believed it, but it is the truth. I watched a video recording of the dust down played later on a television monitor in a Belfast courtroom. The morning after the fight, two UVF men called at Gowdy's home in Ballyclare and told him Haddock wanted to see him at the Monkstown Social Club. One of them, whom Gowdy knew well, instructed him to get into their car. Gowdy declined and told them he would follow behind in his own car. During the drive from Ballyclare to Monkstown, he watched the man he knew using his mobile a lot in the car in front. More than likely he was ringing Haddock to tell him Gowdy was on his way. After the twenty-minute drive the two cars pulled into the car park at the social club.

Haddock appeared from behind a wall. He told Gowdy that if he had been at the pub the previous night, he would have hanged him from a tree for hitting some of his men. Without further warning, Haddock struck Gowdy over the head with an iron bar. Most people would never have recovered from such a blow, but Gowdy was as strong as a bull and fought back, punching Haddock in the face and knocking him to the ground. But Gowdy was outnumbered by Haddock's men which included Haddock's best friend, Darren Moore. They unleashed a vicious and sustained assault on Gowdy, attacking him with iron bars, knives and a hatchet. This act of savagery on another Protestant took place in broad daylight outside a loyalist drinking club. It showed yet again that Haddock and his crowd were not worried about who witnessed such deeds as they had the Special Branch on their side.

They put a bloodied and battered Gowdy into the boot of a car and like a scene from the movie *Goodfellas*, they stabbed Gowdy several times with knives and hit him again with their iron bars. With the boot closed, Haddock and his team were ready to drive off to another location with a plan to kill him. In the darkness of the boot, Gowdy tried to use his mobile phone to raise the alarm. He heard one of the gang say: 'We'll dump him where we dumped McCord.' It was a clear reference to the murder of my son and the plan was to abandon Gowdy at Ballyduff quarry which wasn't too far from the social club. Haddock's gang overheard Gowdy on his mobile and stopped the car. When they opened the boot, Gowdy fought for his life, kicking and punching. He was able to get away from his attackers, but only for a short distance as one of his legs gave way. It was in fact broken, the fracture caused by the force of the hatchet blow. The man who had swung the hatchet was another Special Branch informant. As Trevor lay in the car park, Haddock dragged him behind a wall and hit him again several times with an iron bar and told him he would die there.

Believing Gowdy was finished, Haddock and his thugs left the champion boxer in a crumpled heap with blood pouring from his head, torso and limbs. Lady luck, however, was on Trevor's side for he woke up in hospital. This was a brave man who had survived a brutal attempt on his life by a gang of thugs who were also registered police informants. It was to be the start of Haddock's downfall and the unmasking of his gang. His brigadier Rab Warnock and the UVF leadership on the Shankill Road had turned a blind eye to another attack on a Protestant during its supposed ceasefire. When the assault became public knowledge, the word on the grapevine in Newtownabbey and north Belfast was that the murder bid was the work of Haddock and members of his Mount Vernon UVF. The police made a number of arrests, but it appeared they were only going through the motions again as Haddock was on their payroll.

Eventually the people of that community would hear of a welcome breakthrough in the investigation into Haddock and his mob. Trevor Gowdy, who was still recovering from his horrific injuries, decided enough was enough and made a signed statement to the police, naming several of his attackers including convicted UVF terrorist David 'Reggie' Millar. When the police raided Haddock's Mount Vernon home, they found the front door open. It was left open so that the police would not have to sledge hammer their way in, thus damaging the door. But Haddock had already taken flight and the suspicion was that he had been tipped off in advance, possibly by his handler, about the planned raid. I later learned from police officers that if they wanted to carry out arrests or searches, the operations had to be cleared in advance first by the Special Branch to allow them to tip off their informants and ensure their houses were clear of any guns or drugs. In reality, it bought the Special Branch some time if they needed to tip off a source and alert them to a possible arrest and search operation. The clearing office for all such requests was known as '2-20', based at Castlereagh Police Station.

As part of the Gowdy investigation, the police also searched the home of Darren Moore and found his back door also lying open so that the police could walk in without causing any damage. To know that the PSNI were so considerate when it came to arresting killers who were informers was indeed touching! Maybe the police believed the killers could not afford to have new doors fitted so they would ask them to leave them unlocked during attempts to find them.

Now both Haddock and Moore were on the run. North Belfast was awash with the rumour that Haddock was living in a little village just outside Belfast. The newspapers named the village, yet the PSNI couldn't seem to find it, never mind arrest Haddock. He was also able to slip back into Mount Vernon several times to visit friends and family without being arrested. Perhaps the police were short of manpower on these occasions and were unable to capture him.

Darren 'Judas' Moore was eventually arrested in east Belfast and was charged with the attempted murder of Trevor Gowdy. I was told by my sources that Haddock had left Northern Ireland and was living in Wales with Terry Fairfield, a former member of Mount Vernon UVF. To my amazement, I was told that Fairfield was not only a Special Branch informant but he was also a Catholic. I was staggered at hearing this because Mount Vernon UVF murdered men, women and children just because they were Catholics, and here we had a Catholic from the republican New Lodge Road among its members. Several times the PSNI were told that Haddock was staying at Fairfield's pub in Wales.

Then one evening I received a call from a journalist who asked me to stay quiet on the information he had. It seemed that within hours of Moore's arrest the PSNI suddenly became aware of where Haddock was staying. The information given to me was that Haddock would be arrested within days. So much for the loyalty of friends, as Haddock would later find out to his cost. On the night of his arrest, it was widely rumoured that he was caught by the

Raymond Snr's football team, Star of the Sea under-16s, 1969. Bobby Sands is in the front row, circled, with Raymond Snr behind, circled. (*Conor McCaughley*)

Raymond Snr and his three sons at Christmas 1983, with Santa Claus. (*Left to right*) Glenn, Raymond, Gareth.

Raymond Jnr (left) and Gareth at bedtime.

A smiling Raymond Jnr at primary school, 1984.

Raymond Jnr and Gareth leaving home for primary school, 1985.

Raymond Jnr (back row, in blue) with school football friends.

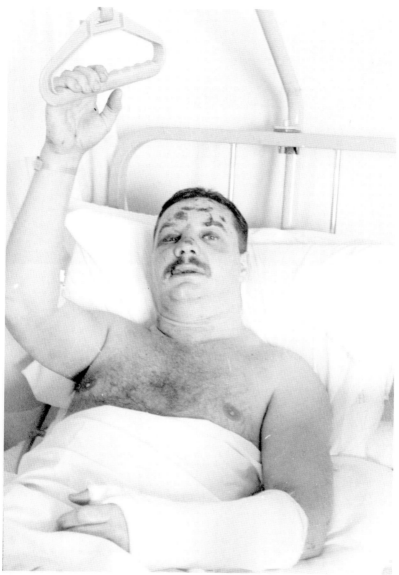

Raymond Snr in hospital recovering from an attack by a mob of UDA thugs, February 1992. His face is swollen like the Elephant Man after flagstones were dropped on both his face and body. (*Conor McCaughley*)

Raymond Snr holidaying in Spain with his youngest son Glenn (the footballer), 1997.

Raymond Jnr in happier days.

Carrying Raymond Jnr's coffin on the heartbreaking day of his funeral, 14 November 1997. (*Conor McCaughley*)

A UVF thug from Mount Vernon.

The result of one of three attacks on Raymond Jnr's headstone by the UVF, 1999. (*Conor McCaughley*)

Mount Vernon UVF, with police informant Mark Haddock second from left, 2000.

Raymond Snr and his friend the late John Niblock (*extreme right*) with Secretary of State John Reid, in the *Sunday World* office, 2002.

Raymond Snr with his family: Vivienne, Glenn, Gareth, Debra, at Gareth and Debra's wedding, 2002.

Glenn and his partner Jacqueline on holiday in Greece, 2004.

Raymond Snr holding his granddaughter Leah at her christening party in the Thunderdome café, Newtownabbey, 2006.

Raymond Snr and granddaughter Nicole enjoying the sun, 2006.

Raymond Snr asking Gerry Adams what he intended to do about the O'Loan report, January 2007. (*Conor McCaughley*)

Raymond Snr with a group of relatives of victims in Washington, March 2007.

Raymond Snr in a bar in New York, St Patrick's Day 2007.

Raymond Snr in 'Cheers' bar in Boston, 2007.

Raymond Snr speaking in the European Parliament building in Strasbourg, April 2007.

Raymond Snr with his grandson Dylan Raymond McCord, September 2007.

Raymond Snr and the Police Ombudsman for Northern Ireland, Nuala O'Loan, in Boston at the IAUC conference, October 2007.

police in Wales sitting in Fairfield's jeep. Not long after his arrest I was phoned by a reliable source and told of the development. I immediately rang Newtownabbey CID and spoke to an acting detective inspector. When I put it to him about Haddock's arrest, he was baffled and told me it was the first he had heard of it and would check it out. Half an hour later I rang him and he confirmed an arrest had been made in Wales but he would not say who it was. Yet again my sources had proved reliable, but I was astounded that the acting detective inspector, who was also involved in my son's murder investigation, had been kept in the dark about Haddock's arrest. It didn't say much for the integrity of senior policemen when a civilian like myself knew about Haddock's arrest before the local CID detectives who were supposed to be looking for him. The following day Haddock was flown back to Belfast and appeared in court, charged with the attempted murder of Trevor Gowdy and other serious offences, including kidnapping.

For Trevor Gowdy the nightmare was getting worse. The UVF couldn't get to him, so they targeted his family. From his prison cell and in a desperate attempt to silence his victim, Haddock ordered attacks to be carried out on the homes of Gowdy's relatives, including that of his girlfriend. Gun and bomb attacks were used to intimidate them in the hope of persuading Gowdy to withdraw his statement. UVF munitions were being used yet again, even though they were supposed to be on ceasefire, and the organisation's leadership did nothing to stop it. The silence from Unionist politicians on these attacks on Gowdy's family was almost deafening. At no time did they call for the arrest of the UVF leaders, as they would have done if these attacks had been carried out by the IRA. I have no doubt they would have called for the arrest of Sinn Féin leader Gerry Adams. No

Unionist politician was calling for the arrest of David Ervine, the UVF's political mouthpiece and a convicted bomber. Democracy was being attacked with UVF threats, shootings and bombings against the Gowdy family, yet no one was arrested.

Trevor Gowdy was powerless to do anything to protect his family. After spending months in hospital under armed police guard, the PSNI moved him to England and put him on a witness protection scheme. But I have found out that in situations like this, when your family and friends are under threat from the likes of Haddock's mob, you have to bend the law a little and pay them a visit. It's amazing how their attitude changes when you arrive at their door not bearing gifts; they start to whistle a different tune.

With Trevor Gowdy now safely in England, the UVF intensified their attempts to get to him through his family and friends. They murdered his best friend John 'Jock' Allen from Ballyclare. One night in November 2003, two UVF men arrived at his second-floor flat at Rashee Park to try and find out where Gowdy was living. According to the report, Jock, who was aged 31, had made up his mind that he was not going down without a fight. A UVF leadership source is quoted in the report as saying: 'They weren't expecting him to come out fighting. As soon as they got into the flat, Jock was waiting for them. He refused to tell them where Gowdy was living. But something went badly wrong. Their orders were to shoot him in both legs as a punishment. Instead they shot him twice in the head.' It seemed to me that Jock Allen, like Trevor Gowdy, knew how to use his hands when he needed to, and was not prepared to bow down to threats and intimidation from the UVF in Ballyclare. My belief is that he was shot dead for two reason: (1) he was Trevor Gowdy's best friend, and (2) he was a brave man who was prepared to stand up to the uvf. To his family I say don't give up on justice just yet.

During the whole time Mark Haddock was on the run, the police didn't issue a single photograph of him, even though it was common knowledge throughout the loyalist areas of Belfast that the police were looking for him. Then one day a journalist, David Gordon from the *Belfast Telegraph*, phoned and asked to meet me. At the meeting he produced a photograph of Haddock. All David wanted was for me to confirm that it was in fact Haddock. With the greatest of pleasure I confirmed his identity. The following day, 20 August 2003, the picture was splashed across the front page of the *Belfast Telegraph*. It was the first time his face had been seen in a newspaper. Martin O'Hagan and John Cassidy, both journalists with the *Sunday World*, had written about Haddock, 'a callous and ruthless uvf informer', many times over the years since young Raymond's murder, but this was the first time the public were able to see what he looked like. There would be no more hiding for him.

One of the most sickening points regarding Haddock, as far as I was concerned, was that even though in 2003 Hugh Orde had been Chief Constable of the psni for a year, he had still not dismissed Haddock as an informant — this despite the fact that he was working on the Stevens Inquiry investigating collusion between the security forces and loyalist paramilitaries into the murder of Belfast solicitor Pat Finucane. I had written a letter to the Stevens team about Haddock's role as a police informant and the fact that he had been involved in a number of murders. Sir Hugh Orde has confirmed to me that he was aware of the letter and that it was passed on to the office of the then Chief Constable Sir Ronnie Flanagan who has said that he never saw the letter. Haddock continued to work as a police informant for over a year after Orde's appointment and was an informer when he tried to murder Trevor Gowdy. He was still an informer when the Police Ombudsman's office communicated its concerns about problems relating to informant handling to the chief constable in a meeting on 25 March 2003, and again on other occasions. For twelve years, from 1991 to 2003, Haddock was controlled by the Special Branch as an informant, was involved in at least ten murders and was paid a minimum of £80,000 of taxpayers' money for his 'work'. He was not the only one within Mount Vernon UVF who had murdered people and were never held accountable due to the fact that they were informants. But none of this should have come as any surprise to the police, who knew full well the pedigrees of Haddock and his associates and their lengthy involvement in terrorism and serious crime.

When Haddock was sentenced at Belfast Crown Court in November 2006 for the attack on Trevor Gowdy, I was shocked to hear the extent of his criminal record read to the trial judge. The prosecution lawyer said he had fifty-four previous convictions, several for grievous bodily harm for which he received suspended sentences. At the time of those convictions he was a Special Branch informer. I am sure his Special Branch minders would have gladly supplied any prospective employer with good 'character references' for Haddock if he needed one. I cannot understand how any law enforcement agency in the world would employ a murderer, a drug dealer and an extortionist with so many criminal convictions and claim it is for the greater good to have this animal working for them. Only the Special Branch in Northern Ireland would do it, I believe.

The attack on Trevor Gowdy brought Haddock's reign of terror to an end but his trial and that of his UVF associates was a farce. My family and friends attended the court proceedings. We wanted to show the courtroom, packed with uvf thugs, that there were people in Northern Ireland who weren't afraid of them. The first day of the trial became bogged down in legal arguments between the prosecution and the defence, so we left. When the trial was in full swing and when Trevor Gowdy was due to give evidence, we went back to the court to give Trevor moral support. The psni had ringed the court inside and out with officers, and just before the case was about to start, the police called me out to inform me that they had information that I was going to be attacked inside or outside the court. Bring it on! Make my day! I noticed that Willie Young was in court. He took the seat furthest from me.

By this time the whole country knew about the activities of the Mount Vernon uvf and Haddock thanks to the *Sunday World*, *Sunday Life*, the *Belfast Telegraph* and Ulster Television, who were constantly highlighting young Raymond's case. In 2004, when the *Sunday World* published a photograph of five hooded men in paramilitary uniform carrying rifles and machine guns, the public started to pay attention. The *Sunday World* went a step further than other newspapers and named the hooded men. One of the five was Haddock. The picture showed a man lying on the ground whom the newspaper named as Willie 'Mr Muscles' Young, who killed Raymond with a breeze block. To him I say, I'm confident my life span will be longer than yours, Willie.

As the courtroom was packed with uvf men, I took the seat nearest their supporters. If I was going to be hurt, then some of them would not be going home in the condition they arrived. I had my two best friends with me, my sons Gareth and Glenn, and believe me we were ready for anything the scum would try. I could feel the adrenalin pumping through my veins and my heart beating faster.

When the court rose for lunch, we made a point of standing close to the exit so that they would have to walk past us. Not one of the yellow-bellied bastards would look us in the eye. Their motto of 'For God and Ulster' was now 'Get me out quick. There's the McCords!' This was the so-called cream of Mount Vernon UVF in court supporting police informants. Maybe their handlers told them to attend.

The trial was subsequently adjourned due to the ill-health of the star witness Trevor Gowdy, but what disgusted all the decent people in court was that Haddock sat smirking in the dock the whole time Gowdy was describing to the trial judge, Mr Justice Ronald Weatherup, the gruesome details of the attack outside the Monkstown Social Club where Warnock and the UVF drank. Haddock must have believed this was going to be another occasion when his Special Branch handlers would step in and save the day for him. I noticed that on one of the occasions he was smirking, Mr Justice Weatherup looked over at him and took note of his expression.

During his account Trevor Gowdy broke down once or twice, which was quite understandable as he relived that night again. It must have felt extremely uncomfortable in the witness box, as the ringleader of those who had attacked him sat just feet away with a large grin on his face. If it had not been for his bravery and fighting ability, he would have been brutally murdered. All I can say is fair play to Trevor, because he got through it where lesser men wouldn't have had the courage to stand up to Haddock and his mob. Someday I will shake Trevor Gowdy's hand, buy him a pint, and if I can help him in any way, I will.

We thought Trevor's evidence would convict all the defendants. But I was astounded when only Haddock and one other, Darren Moore, were left in the dock. One of his co-accused, Reggie Millar, another Special Branch informant, was set free even though Trevor had picked him out from an identification parade as the man with the hatchet. It was claimed that the police had not checked his alibi at the time of the attack, that he was in a bank. Poor police work or what! I was arrested in the past for allegedly assaulting paramilitaries without any weapons and I wasn't released from custody until my alibi was checked out and verified. There must be different laws for UVF men than for the rest of us. Moore was free as there was not enough evidence to proceed against him. The judge told the police that if they wanted to pursue the case against Moore, they would have to gather more evidence. Strangely, the police haven't produced any more evidence against him.

Towards the end of the trial the number of UVF supporters attending the hearing was falling off. I believe some at long last were finally accepting that Haddock was an informant, which is what I had told the UVF leadership back in November 1997. It indicated the efficiency of the UVF's internal security team if it had taken them nearly a decade to wise up to Haddock. I still wonder if they ever finished their inquiry into the £1 million worth of drugs found in Mount Vernon in 1999. With Haddock occupying the dock on his own, the UVF decided to move against him. He was put off the UVF wing in Maghaberry Prison and had to be housed in a segregation unit. His only friend was Clifford McKeown, a former UVF supergrass, also housed in the segregated unit.

When Moore went up the Shankill Road to complain, he was told to sling his hook. The message from the leadership was loud and clear, that Haddock had now been ditched. He was *persona non grata*. I thought that with Haddock no longer able to wield his power, the threats on me would stop.

But they didn't. In fact the threats, and their frequency, increased.

Haddock wasn't the only one thrown to the wolves. The UVF had also decided to remove Rab Warnock as the south east Antrim brigadier, the 'drunken brigadier' as the *Sunday World* regularly referred to him. He and his second-in-command, Billy Greer, got the boot for ripping off the UVF leadership to the tune of £500,000 in drug money. The pair didn't realise that a man being groomed to be the next brigadier, Gary 'Cowhead' Haggarty, was reporting back to the UVF's chief of staff John 'Bunter' Graham that they were skimming money from the top UVF heads. When Warnock was stood down, Haggarty was sworn in as brigadier. He was another PSNI Special Branch informer and the man the police believed who shot dead grandfather Sean McParland in Skegoneil, north Belfast, in 1994. He was one of a dozen UVF men convicted over the attack on the Golden Hind pub in Portadown several years later. After a while I began to realise that the person making the threats on me was Haggarty himself. I also have reliable information that he was the one who smashed young Raymond's headstone on one of the three occasions it was targeted. I haven't forgotten that, Cowhead. After finding out he was behind the threats on me, I decided to pay him a house call and sat outside his house. But big man and all that he was, he would not come to the door. Instead he would peer out through his blinds. He also discovered that walking could be dangerous for his health as he carried a bit of extra weight, not just in his wallet from his illegal money-making rackets, but also around his belly and his heart. He might have had a big belly, but he had no guts when it came to a one on one with me or one of my sons.

In May 2006 I was sitting on a beach on holiday when I received a text message. It said that Haddock had been shot five or six times and everyone thought he was going to die. It was the card the UVF played to show he was finished. But Haddock survived the shooting. Yet again David Ervine jumped to the defence of the UVF. He told the media it was the work of 'opportunists' and not the UVF. He sounded like a broken record every time he was interviewed. In his eyes the UVF never did anything wrong and were being wrongly blamed for things they didn't do. He trotted out the same old tripe time and time again and certain gullible sections of the media bought it hook, line and sinker and never questioned the UVF's so-called ceasefire of October 1994. But I didn't hear too much more from Ervine when Haddock made a statement to PSNI detectives and named two of the three people involved. Those he named were his best mate Darren 'Judas' Moore and Ronnie 'Poof' Bowe, another UVF man who was a former Irish amateur champion boxer and who was convicted over the Golden Hind pub attack. They were both arrested and charged with attempted murder and remanded in custody. A car used in the shooting was found burned out not far away. It belonged to Moore's girlfriend. Here we had two known UVF guys from Mount Vernon 3rd battalion charged with attempted murder, a car belonging to the girlfriend of one of those charged used as a getaway vehicle, and we had David Ervine saying the UVF didn't do it. I believe he did himself and the UVF more harm than good by repeatedly telling lies about their activities. When did David Ervine *ever* say that the UVF killed a Protestant?

There was a third person involved whom Haddock didn't name, Willie Young. On the day of the shooting, this is what happened, I was told. Gary Haggarty received orders from the UVF leadership to kill Haddock. Haggarty would take great pleasure in this as he hated Haddock after he had once been beaten up by him. Haggarty met with Willie Young, his co in Mount Vernon, and told him Haddock had to be taken out at a meeting which was just a cover to get close to him. Darren 'Judas' Moore, Haddock's best friend and the one he thought he could trust, was used as the bait. Moore rang Haddock and asked to meet him. At the meeting Moore and Bowe got out of their car and, as Haddock approached, Bowe shot him with his .22 gun five or six times. Moore and Bowe jumped back into the car which Willie Young was driving. I believe Haddock never named Young because 'Mr Muscles' knew too many of Haddock's secrets and he couldn't risk him telling all to the police. However, Moore and Bowe didn't spend too long on remand when Haddock retracted his statement and the charges against the pair were dropped. I believe he did a deal with the UVF. He would drop the charges against Moore and Bowe if the UVF allowed his mum and stepfather to live in peace in Mount Vernon.

To this day none of the 'opportunists' has been punished by the UVF. There was no inquiry as to why UVF guns were used in the shooting. My personal opinion is that the UVF and David Ervine wanted the whole Haddock shooting to go away as quickly as possible because Young, Moore and Bowe had made such a mess of the murder bid. It was a case of least said, soonest mended, as far as Ervine and the UVF were concerned. I don't want supporters of David Ervine reading this to think I am speaking ill of the dead. I am not. I am just quoting his own words and statements truthfully — unlike what he said about my son Raymond. The difference between us is that I tell the truth about the dead; others say what the UVF tells them.

With Haddock in the intensive care unit of the Royal Victoria Hospital in Belfast under police protection and fighting for his life, another chapter in my life had closed and we as a family no longer had to prove that he was an agent of the State, a highly paid police informant. The UVF leadership knew all along that I had been telling the truth. Even before the shooting, Haddock and his cronies had been well and truly unmasked with great support from the media who believed in me, and also great determination from my family who wanted to uncover the truth about my son's savage murder.

When judgment day finally arrived for Haddock, Gareth and I made sure we had front row seats in the public gallery of the court. We both wanted to see Haddock's face. I was hoping to get close enough to bid him goodbye my way. The coward didn't attend the court in person. Instead he appeared by video link from Maghaberry Prison. He looked like an old man. The attempt on his life had finished him. And for all the power he once commanded in Mount Vernon, only three people turned up to support him. Even his long-time girlfriend Helen McAllister, the daughter of former UVF life sentence prisoner William McAllister, also failed to show. The rats had deserted the sinking ship. Mr Justice Weatherup found Haddock guilty of causing grievous bodily harm with intent, kidnapping and arson.

Haddock's sentence of ten years for destroying Trevor Gowdy's life was pathetic. I wonder what sentence the judge would have given Haddock if it had been his own son Haddock had brutally attacked. Outside the court I told the assembled reporters what I thought of the sentence. It was disgraceful and he should have been given life. The judge was aware that Haddock had fifty-four previous convictions, some of which were for causing grievous bodily harm. It wouldn't have surprised me if someone in the Special Branch had written a letter to the judiciary, pointing out his previous work for the State in the hope that he would get a reduced sentence.

At the time of writing, Haddock is still in Maghaberry Prison, segregated from other UVF inmates for his own safety. With time served on remand and also the 50 per cent remission that all prisoners receive in Northern Ireland, he is expected to be released within the next year. I hope some day to catch up with him and have that little chat with no one about, just him and me. To my son Raymond I promise that.

10.
Operation Ballast

I had exhausted every avenue that I could think of that could help in my search for the truth about young Raymond's murder. It was now four and a half years since he was brutally killed and I was still angry and frustrated that those responsible were still walking the streets.

The RUC had let me and my family down as they knew who killed Raymond, yet the Special Branch was protecting the killers because they were registered agents, so-called 'assets of the State'. These bloodthirsty murderers were a law unto themselves. They killed freely in north Belfast and in return were paid handsome sums of cash by their Special Branch handlers for passing on information about terrorist activity in the area. I was sickened by what I had uncovered during my own investigation and wanted it to stop.

I was walking through Belfast city centre one day in May 2002 thinking about how I could push forward Raymond's case and expose the dirty dealings I had uncovered between the UVF in north Belfast and the RUC Special Branch. I was walking up Donegall Street near St Anne's Cathedral. Directly in front of me was a large brick building which

housed the offices of the Police Ombudsman for Northern
Ireland. I had passed it many times before, but on this day I
decided I would make a formal complaint about the RUC's
handling of my son's murder. This was a spur of the moment
decision to see if the Police Ombudsman could get me truth
and justice.

A security guard buzzed me in. I had no idea of the
formalities involved or how to go about it. I asked if I could
speak to the lady in charge, the Police Ombudsman herself,
Nuala O'Loan. Two minutes later a woman stepped out of a
lift, came into the foyer and introduced herself as Mrs
O'Loan's secretary. She told me that Mrs O'Loan would see
me right away. I was genuinely surprised as I didn't have an
appointment. Little did I realise then that my complaint
would open a Pandora's box of collusion and cover-up
between the forces of law and order in Northern Ireland and
a loyalist paramilitary organisation. I thought this type of
collusion between State forces and guerrilla outfits only
happened in Third World countries or dictatorships.

I was shown into Mrs O'Loan's fourth-floor office for a
private meeting just between the two of us. We shook hands,
introduced ourselves and we sat down at her desk. I was a bit
nervous because this was new territory for me, but I had to
do something for young Raymond and the Police
Ombudsman was probably my last chance of getting justice
for him. I explained to her the details surrounding the
murder of my son at the hands of the UVF, and that my own
enquiries had shown that some of those involved were
working as RUC Special Branch informants who I believed
were being protected from prosecution by the Special
Branch. I told her I was given little or no information about
the progress of the RUC investigation and that I believed there
was a cover-up between certain Special Branch handlers and

their informants. I also explained to her that I had been told that a number of UVF men, both senior and junior, were involved in at least a dozen murders. I said they were also involved, to my knowledge, in drug dealing, extortion, bombings, possession of explosives, guns and ammunition, hijackings, intimidation and serious assaults. My list went on and on. I told her that the majority of these UVF men were informants for the Special Branch and were able to carry out these crimes without any fear of being prosecuted as the Special Branch made sure they remained on the streets.

What I told Mrs O'Loan was to form the four central planks of my formal complaint against the RUC. These were that:

(1) a senior UVF man, Mark Haddock, the commanding officer of Mount Vernon, had ordered the murder of my son and he was a police informant;

(2) the police had failed to carry out a thorough investigation into Raymond's murder and had failed to keep me up to date about the progress of their investigation;

(3) no one had been arrested or charged with Raymond's murder because Mark Haddock was a police informant and those working for Haddock had been protected from arrest and prosecution for a number of years; and

(4) unidentified police knew something was going to happen to Raymond but did not warn him or my family about the danger in order to protect Haddock who was responsible for my son's murder.

I was making serious allegations to the Police Ombudsman about misconduct by the RUC and in particular those in the Special Branch who handled informants. I had always been led to believe that the role of an informant was to provide intelligence in advance of an attack so that lives could be saved. But from what I was being told by my contacts over the previous five years, this was not happening within north Belfast UVF and within the wider south east Antrim brigade. I had set Mrs O'Loan and her team a daunting task to either substantiate or dismiss my allegations.

For a few months I let the Police Ombudsman forge ahead with her investigation. Then I started to contact her to find out what was going on. I needed to know how it was progressing because I was pinning my hopes on her team getting to the heart of the matter. I was told she was making progress, but it was slow and there was some opposition to her getting the information she needed to push on with her investigation. She knew the information existed, but the Special Branch were reluctant to divulge it. To me it appeared they had something to hide. I remember something that was said during the so-called RUC 'shoot-to-kill' controversy in the 1980s, that the Special Branch was a 'force within a force' and it ran the RUC, not the chief constable. I always thought this was republican propaganda to blacken the name of the RUC. Now, as my complaint was being processed, I was beginning to see the truth of that quote. The Special Branch didn't like outsiders poking their noses into their affairs, as others had found before.

As the months passed I was having more regular meetings with Mrs O'Loan and her head of investigations Dave Wood, a tall man with dark hair and glasses who had come from investigating corruption at Scotland Yard in the Metropolitan Police. As I sat listening to what they were telling me, I knew they were starting to uncover a can of worms at the heart of the police in Northern Ireland. What I was being told was confidential. I was not to divulge this information to the media for fear it would jeopardise their investigation, which they called Operation Ballast. But the media already knew as much or more about Mount Vernon UVF from their own sources and the stories about what they uncovered appeared on a weekly basis. The *Sunday World* never shied away from naming those involved and it set down a marker for the rest of the media. The newspaper took great risks, but it believed in me and it believed I was telling the truth.

In 2003 I was informed by Mrs O'Loan that the investigation into my complaint was starting to slow down as she was running out of money to keep it going. I was absolutely furious. I told the media that it was an absolute disgrace that the Northern Ireland Office (NIO) would not give Mrs O'Loan the cash she needed to continue the investigation. I said the British government could find £200 million for the Bloody Sunday Inquiry, and there were further calls to have investigations into the murders of solicitor Rosemary Nelson and Robert Hamill. It appeared to me that the government could find the money to fund inquires into the murders of nationalists and republicans, but Protestants were being excluded. As far as I was concerned, the government should not be putting a price on justice, no matter how uncomfortable it was making certain people in Belfast and London feel. The NIO responded by saying Mrs O'Loan had been provided with the budget she had asked for, and it was up to her to prioritise her resources.

But the NIO had entirely missed the point. My complaint was turning into one of the biggest investigations ever carried out by the Police Ombudsman, even bigger than her report into the August 1998 Omagh bomb atrocity, and she needed the extra resources to cope with the volume of paperwork. There was no mismanagement of resources as far as I knew, and I believed Mrs O'Loan to be a woman of integrity and honesty. After all she was a mother, she understood my hurt and pain and promised to help me. But I believed there were dark forces at work who didn't want her to get at the truth. Too many people, particularly in the police, had too much to lose from Mrs O'Loan's investigation. They knew full well that if she poked in the right corners within the RUC, she could unearth some startling information about the shadowy world of the Special Branch. She was aware from previous reports into terrorist murders — the Omagh atrocity and the murder of GAA official Sean Brown — that the Special Branch had kept back information from the CID, who were trying to catch the killers. There was nothing to suggest that the Special Branch had changed their policy when it came to investigating my son's murder, and it was a near certainty that they had much more to lose from the opening of their intelligence files in my son's case because of the number of informants who were either directly or indirectly involved. The Special Branch had penetrated right to the heart of the UVF and had informants working at every level, right up to the chief of staff. With that many informants on its books, I have often wondered how the UVF were able to kill anyone. Surely it was the job of the Special Branch to frustrate at every opportunity all terrorist activity, to save life and capture those involved.

Or maybe the Special Branch in Northern Ireland had a different attitude in that they just nonchalantly turned a blind eye for the 'greater good' or the 'bigger picture', as they liked to call it. To me, the whole system in Northern Ireland was rotten to the core and the quicker it was exposed, cut out and removed, the better the province would be. If the police force is rotten, with rotten officers at its heart, then who do you turn to for help? The paramilitaries? I don't think so. They acted above the law, while the police acted outside the law. What I have found out over the past decade is that the police were controlling these murder gangs and had the capacity and the resources to close them down and put them behind bars. But they didn't, and it was going to take a working-class man like myself to stand up to them and show the world how they allowed people to kill without any fear of ever being convicted.

During the course of her investigation Mrs O'Loan's team were met with resistance, hostility and obstruction as they went in search of the truth. It was clear to me that certain people inside the police force (including retired officers) were getting nervous about her inquiry. But Mrs O'Loan is a very determined lady and she was not going to be pushed around by bully boy tactics. She had a job to do and she was absolutely determined to get to the bottom of how the police had handled Raymond's murder. I know from some of my earliest conversations with her that she sensed there was something not right with the investigation and was going to leave no stone unturned.

As each year passed I was becoming more and more confident that Mrs O'Loan's determination and steadfastness was paying off. I remember leaving meetings with her and going across to the John Hewitt bar and telling journalists about the progress of the inquiry. All I could say was that some police officers were in trouble and that the report was not going to miss and hit the wall. The news was gradually filtering out that Mrs O'Loan was making headway. The word coming back to me was that some officers, particularly those in the Special Branch, were getting uneasy about the report. I was even told that certain sections of the RUC were ready to go on the offensive against Mrs O'Loan to rubbish the report even before it was published. They were going to try and blacken her name in the hope that it would discredit the report. I had also been reliably informed that some

Unionist politicians, who were known to be sympathetic to the RUC and knew what wrongdoing they had got up to, were also being lined up to knock the report. That heartened me because I knew then that the police were getting rattled big time and that Mrs O'Loan was doing her job. However, young Raymond's murder remained unsolved and the killers remained at large enjoying their freedom. But each new year brought the hope that this would be the year the report would be completed.

During my search for justice and truth I met many political figures. At one time I said I didn't wish to speak to the Irish Taoiseach Bertie Ahern. My reason was that he should have nothing to do with what was happening in Northern Ireland. I was wrong, but I still believed that the British government gave the Irish government too much of a say in Northern Ireland's political affairs and problems. Yet when I met Ahern, I was greatly impressed by him.

My visit to Dublin to see Bertie Ahern was not my first trip across the border to raise the profile of my son's case and let the people of the Republic hear a Protestant's story about state collusion with loyalist paramilitaries in the murder of a Protestant. I had been there some months before to see the leader of the Irish Labour Party, Pat Rabbitte. The person who made that possible was Mark Langhammer, an old friend of mine who knew Raymond. Mark is one of the most genuine people I've come across in my quest. Political leaders in Northern Ireland should look at Mark and open their eyes to see how much he has to offer the two communities in Northern Ireland. Like me, he doesn't give a damn what religion a person is. He should have been given a job at Stormont to work with victims or to help promote cross-community projects, as he has the expertise.

When Mark accompanied me down to Dublin for my first

visit, I really didn't know what to expect. However, Pat Rabbitte listened attentively to me and when I had finished he asked me what I wanted him to do for Raymond's case. I told him that I needed help in exposing the killers and Mark Haddock's role as an informer for the Special Branch. Rabbitte had some serious matters to consider. When I left him and his party colleagues, he assured me that I would hear from him in the near future as he had so much to digest and consider. Unlike Unionist politicians, he did come back to me through Mark with the news that he would be raising the matter in the Dáil, the Irish parliament. When that day came, on 27 October 2005, I sat in the public gallery of the Dáil with a lump in my throat when I heard Pat Rabbitte talk about Raymond's murder. It was all I could do not to break down and cry. The tough guy from north Belfast was almost reduced to tears. Pat's words were fantastic. He said:

Mr McCord has suffered a campaign of intimidation and violence from the UDA. He has been beaten up and left for dead. Subsequently, he has campaigned to obtain justice for his son. Gunmen have targeted his family and he has been ordered to leave Northern Ireland. He has refused to do so. I salute both his courage and integrity.

Perhaps it was in order to seek protection from the UDA that his son became involved briefly with Mount Vernon UVF under the command of Mark Haddock. In November 1997 he was battered to death and his body dumped in a quarry. According to his father, Mount Vernon UVF murdered Raymond McCord because he had been summoned by John 'Bunter' Graham, the OC of the UVF on the Shankill Road, to account for his role in ferrying drugs for Mark Haddock. He was murdered to prevent Graham finding out about Haddock's unsanctioned drugs operation.

At least two members of the gang who carried out the murder were Special Branch informers. They were Mark Haddock who ordered the murder, and John Bond who was present when Raymond McCord was murdered. The central allegation is that Mark Haddock was not charged with any crime because he was an informer who had to be protected. He was able to act with impunity while the police effectively colluded in his crimes.

For almost eight years the investigation into the Raymond McCord case has gone nowhere. His father is morally certain who killed his son, but the perpetrators enjoy immunity for their acts. The police need for intelligence had trumped the State's duty to protect the right to life. Mark Haddock is now awaiting trial for attempted murder.

Pat Rabbitte called for a 'comprehensive and credible inquiry' into Raymond's murder, which needed to have an international element in order to guarantee independence and impartiality.

The Irish Labour Party leader finished his Dáil address by saying: 'Finally, Mr Raymond McCord has lost a 22-year-old son to a violent and ruthless organisation that seems to have operated with the surreptitious sanction of the police. We owe it to him and to all others who have lost family, friends and neighbours to ensure, as best we can, that they receive justice.'

I was immensely pleased with Pat Rabbitte's help and will always be indebted to him, to Mark and the other Irish Labour Party colleagues for helping to raise Raymond's case and let the people of the Republic know what happened. I was getting more support for Raymond's case from a country which I had always opposed having a say in the affairs of Northern Ireland. It couldn't get any more bizarre than that.

Despite all this support, I was at times getting somewhat frustrated that it was taking so long for the report to be finished, although I was constantly reassured by Mrs O'Loan and her staff that they had to be sure of what they were going to say in the report and that every 't' had to be crossed and every 'i' dotted. They were not prepared to let anyone punch a hole in the report when it was finally published. I was told to trust them, and that is what I did. The year 2005 ended with the report still unfinished, but 2006 opened with fresh hope that Operation Ballast had not much longer to go. Mrs O'Loan had already sent a file to the Director of Public Prosecutions (DPP) on a number of officers who may have behaved in a criminal way and was awaiting a decision from Sir Alistair Fraser's office. It was clear the politicians sensed Mrs O'Loan was hitting the home straight in her inquiry and questions were being asked. The DUP's East Londonderry MP Gregory Campbell had asked a written question in the House of Commons which stated: '. . . to ask the Secretary of State for Northern Ireland when he expects to receive the Police Ombudsman for Northern Ireland's report on her investigation into the 1997 murder of Raymond McCord Jnr.' The NIO Security Minister Paul Goggins replied: 'The Police Ombudsman has advised that a report of the investigation into matters related to the murder of Raymond McCord Jnr is nearing completion. The Police Ombudsman's investigation is as a result of a complaint from Raymond McCord Snr about the handling of the police investigation of his son's murder, not about the murder itself.' In June, Lady Sylvia Hermon, the Ulster Unionist Party's MP for North

Down, tabled a question asking the Secretary of State Peter Hain if he would meet me after he had previously refused, saying he couldn't because of the forthcoming publication of Mrs O'Loan's report. His answer showed he had a change of heart and replied to Lady Hermon that if she contacted his diary secretary to arrange an appointment, 'I will of course be pleased to see him.' When I met him at Stormont in the presence of Lady Hermon two months later in August, he showed little or no interest in my son's murder. In fact he nodded off at least twice during the meeting. People thought I made this up, but Lady Hermon was with me and saw for herself the disrespect he had shown me. I told the media afterwards that I should have chinned him there and then because I would have happily done three months in jail for the way he treated me. His office would neither confirm nor deny that he fell asleep at our meeting. Maybe his civil servants were not prepared to dig him out of the hole in which he had found himself. I will never forget what he did and I would remind him about it at a future impromptu meeting.

The month of August 2006 was a busy time for Mrs O'Loan's office. I knew she was aiming to have her report done and dusted by the end of the year. There was a possibility it could come out in November, but the likelihood was it would be either at the start of December or January 2007. I didn't think there was much point bringing it out in the run-up to Christmas as I was told it was a quiet news time for the media and the public had little appetite for such news. I wanted the public in Northern Ireland and around the world to hear what Mrs O'Loan had unearthed. Then on the morning of Wednesday, 9 August 2006, I was woken by calls on my mobile phone. Members of the media were ringing to tell me that the Police Ombudsman was carrying out a series of raids in connection with her inquiry into my allegations of collusion between the RUC and the UVF in north Belfast. I turned on the TV and checked both Teletext and Ceefax for further details. I also listened to the radio news which confirmed that two detectives had been arrested for questioning. One of them was retired detective constable Trevor McIlwrath, who I knew had been ill for some time as a result of his work during the Troubles. I was later told he was arrested because he refused to be interviewed voluntarily. His doctor had said he was medically unfit. The news bulletin also said that the home of a third detective in Ballymena, Co. Antrim, was searched and computer equipment and other material taken away for examination. It was the home of Johnston 'Jonty' Brown, a former detective sergeant in the RUC who had written a book about his run-ins with the Special Branch and who was on holiday at the time in Malta. He was later quoted as saying the search came as no surprise to him and he had nothing to hide or fear. Later that Wednesday night he was arrested at Belfast International Airport as he returned from holiday.

The three detectives were arrested on suspicion of perverting the course of justice and for misconduct in public office but were all later released without charge. From my own enquiries, I had been told that Haddock had first been recruited by McIlwrath and Brown as a CID informant way back in the early 1990s when he was involved in criminal behaviour, namely arson and burglary. But once he joined the ranks of the UVF, the CID were told they had to share him with the Special Branch as it had the lead role in the province on gathering intelligence on terrorists. The arrests were a startling development and I had an official phone call from the Ombudsman's office to confirm that the arrests were made in relation to my complaint. I was told the arrests were made because the former officers wouldn't come voluntarily to be interviewed.

What I thought was going to be a quiet summer's day had suddenly gone into overdrive. My mobile and my house phone never stopped all day. The media, my family and friends were all ringing to see if I knew anything more than had already been made public, but I didn't. That weekend the *Sunday World* reported that the Police Ombudsman's office was looking to interview two Special Branch officers in connection with her inquiry. The newspaper named the retired officers as Detective Superintendent Joe Meeke and Detective Sergeant Phil Scott. The *Sunday World* said that Meeke had at one stage been the head of the Special Branch in Belfast who oversaw the running of all informants, and Scott was Mark Haddock's handler. The article said both officers were out of the country at the time of the Operation Ballast raids, with one working as a security adviser in Iraq and the other holidaying in Spain. Both would later be interviewed by the Ombudsman as part of her investigation.

Between September and December I had more private meetings with Mrs O'Loan. She had taken me into her confidence and I would discuss personal issues as they emerged. I was starting to see myself how I thought the report would take shape. From what I had guessed, it was certainly going to make uncomfortable reading for those in the RUC and the UVF who had something to hide. I was no longer feeling frustrated. Mrs O'Loan's team had let no one stand in their way in their search for answers.

I visited young Raymond's grave on the ninth anniversary of his murder, a stronger man. I was able to tell him that the truth would soon be out about who killed him and who protected his killer. I had kept the promise I made to him as I held his hand while he lay in his coffin. And Mrs O'Loan had kept her promise to me that she would search out the truth for my son and my family. I was photographed in that weekend's *Sunday World* laying flowers and tending to Raymond's grave. The UVF had rarely let him rest in peace, but I knew our family's struggle for justice was the right one and now it was finally coming to a conclusion. The UVF had much to lose through my family's determination to get to the truth. Nothing was going to stop us now. We were like a huge juggernaut coming down the hill, gathering pace all the time. We were about to prove to everyone that the McCord family don't lie down easily. We took everything the UVF could throw at us and still bounced back. We took every underhand and every dirty trick in the book the security forces could muster against us, and we were still standing.

I spent Christmas Day at the home of my sons Gareth and Glenn and my grandchildren. They say Christmas is for kids, and there is no bigger kid at Christmas than me. Memories of Christmases Vivienne and I spent with young Raymond and our other two sons were never far from my mind. It was hard not to look at my grandson playing with his toys and not think back to Raymond when he was that age, a happy, carefree little boy. To be honest, Christmas has never been the same without him. We never, ever forgot him; not one of us. Even with all the love and joy that grandchildren can give, there was always something missing from our lives, an empty seat at the table, an empty space in our heart. We were all so close, yet we didn't really know how close we were until he had gone. I am not saying Christmas had lost all its sparkle because I still had my other two sons. It was just that the lights on the Christmas tree seemed that little bit dimmer. But we all knew that young Raymond was looking down on us from above and he was guiding us at every turn.

The New Year brought a new dawn in our lives as we

awaited the publication of the Police Ombudsman's report. I was having meetings nearly every other day with Mrs O'Loan. I had to bring my family in to let her explain how things were going to shape up in the report. I had been told the world's media were coming to Belfast because of the explosive details it contained. At last I had a date for publication. It was going to be released to the press on Monday, 22 January 2007.

The Stormont Hotel's conference facilities in east Belfast had been booked by the Police Ombudsman's staff and a number of private rooms had been set aside for my family if they wanted to be on their own for a while, away from the glare of the TV cameras. In the days before the report's publication, a steady stream of reporters, photographers and camera crew were beating a path to my door. Everybody wanted their readers and viewers to hear my story. I turned no one away because as far as I was concerned these people were just doing their job. As well as that, I wanted as many people as possible around the world to hear that the security forces in Northern Ireland had colluded with the UVF in the murder of both Protestants and Catholics.

In the weeks leading up to the report, I was receiving police messages that loyalist paramilitaries, namely the UVF, were going to take some form of action against me. I was repeatedly warned by Mrs O'Loan to take the threats seriously and I took her advice. I had a number of meetings with the head of the PSNI's Crime Operations Department, Assistant Chief Constable Peter Sheridan, who also advised me to take the threats seriously and not to get complacent as I had received so many threats. He was also concerned that members of the UVF might attempt to attack me in the days before the report was published, and possibly even on the day of publication. I was to get an armed police escort to the hotel as the police were taking no chances with my life. There were people who didn't want me alive when the report was published.

On the Friday before the day of the publication of the report I was in my home with *Sunday World* photographer Conor McCaughley and reporter John Cassidy who were interviewing me for that weekend's newspaper. I pointed out to them what the Ulster Unionist Party peer, Lord Ken Maginnis, was quoted as saying on Teletext. He had rubbished the report before it was even published! How on earth could he rubbish something he hadn't even read? It was ludicrous. But I had been warned to expect a spin campaign to start in the run-up to the publication. Maginnis was not a friend of my family. He never once darkened my door either before or after the publication of the report.

The morning of the report was absolute bedlam. My family had waited for this for five years since I first went to see Mrs O'Loan. In my own mind I had no doubt that I was right in my accusations about Raymond's murder and I was hoping that Mrs O'Loan's investigators would be able to justify them. My health hadn't been the best for some weeks due to a serious back problem. I had been given morphine injections to ease the pain. We all knew it was going to be a long day and this was going to be a big story for the media. Arrangements had been made for me and my solicitor Paul Farrell to meet Mrs O'Loan and her senior staff at the Police Ombudsman's headquarters off Donegall Street at around 7.30 a.m. As Nuala O'Loan explained the main points of the report to us, I experienced both joy and sadness, joy that Haddock and the police were going to be exposed to the world, and sadness that our lovely son had been murdered in the first place.

Nuala O'Loan and her team had done everything they

possibly could to make things as gentle as possible. The care and consideration they showed was a credit to their office and I will never forget that. Looking back now, everything seemed to move so fast. Not long after my solicitor and I were briefed, Vivienne, Gareth and Glenn arrived to be given the same briefing. I knew Vivienne would be all right as Gareth and Glenn were with her.

The report did not name the individuals involved; they were identified by numbers and letters. The full report, warts and all, had been given to the PSNI Chief Constable Sir Hugh Orde and the Secretary of State Peter Hain. It identified the informants and police officers who were central to my complaint. However, because of legal constraints, I was only allowed to read the report released to the media and the public. The report was devastating to read, but I could not make any notes and was not allowed to contact anyone about its content prior to publication. Mrs O'Loan's staff sat with me in the room with the report to make sure I conformed to her request. It was a huge report, about the thickness of a telephone book, and it ran to 160 pages. I tried to take in as much as I could, but there was a veritable mountain of facts and figures. But I was right. Mark Haddock was a tout and he ordered my son's murder. That could not be denied.

Flicking through the weighty tome, I turned to the chapter headed 'Conclusions'. Even though the informants were not named, I knew who Mrs O'Loan was writing about. I hadn't come this far not to know who the touts were. The chapter read as follows:

Conclusions of the Police Ombudsman about the allegations made by Mr Raymond McCord about the death of his son

Allegation 1: that a senior UVF figure had ordered

the murder of his son, and that this individual was a police informant. Finding: The Police Ombudsman can confirm that a police informant is a suspect in the murder of Mr McCord's son. She cannot confirm or deny who that individual is.

Allegation 2: that police had failed to carry out a thorough investigation of his son's murder and had failed to keep him updated about their investigation. Findings: The Police Ombudsman has identified failures in the investigation of Mr McCord's son's murder. These failures may have significantly reduced the possibility of anyone being prosecuted for murder. There is some material which indicates some contact between specific police officers and Mr McCord, particularly during the days immediately following the murder. There has been a failure by those supervising the conduct of the police investigation to consider the benefit of identifying at the very least a single point of contact with Mr McCord. Such provision may have allowed the investigation to progress more effectively. The allegation is substantiated.

Allegation 3: that no one had been arrested or charged with the murder of his son. Mr McCord alleged that this was because the man who ordered the murder was a police informant, and that this individual, and those working for him, had been protected from arrest and prosecution for a number of years. Findings: A number of people were arrested for Raymond McCord Junior's murder. No one has been charged with the murder. There is no evidence that anyone has been protected from arrest for the murder of Raymond McCord Junior. With reference to Mr McCord's allegation that a police informant had

ordered his son's murder, and that this individual and
those working for him had been protected from arrest
and prosecution for years, the Police Ombudsman
conducted an extensive investigation which is detailed
in this report. It is clear that much intelligence was
disregarded by police and that they continued to use
Informant 1 despite his criminal record and the
extensive intelligence they held in respect of alleged
serious criminality, because he had value to them as an
informant. This was wrong. This allegation is therefore
substantiated with the exception firstly, of that part of
it which refers to the police failure to arrest anyone for
Raymond McCord Junior's murder, and secondly, of
the fact that, whilst the Police Ombudsman can
confirm that an informer is a suspect in the murder of
Mr McCord's son, she cannot confirm or deny who
that individual is.

Allegation 4: that unidentified police knew
something was going to happen to Raymond McCord
Junior, but that they did not warn him or his family
about the danger to protect the police informant who
was responsible for the murder. Finding: The Police
Ombudsman has found no evidence or intelligence to
support this allegation. It is not substantiated.

Two of my complaints had been substantiated and one
part of a third complaint. In the fourth, no evidence or
intelligence was found to substantiate it, but as far as I was
concerned it didn't mean it didn't exist. Remember, this was
the Special Branch who in the eyes of many, including rank
and file police, ran the RUC. But the more I read of the
confidential report, the more my adrenalin increased. I had
waited for over nine years to find out what happened to my

son, and now I had a report into his murder and I was finding it so hard to take in everything. It was like being put in a sweet shop and being told you could have anything you wanted. But where do you start: at the front, the middle or the end? It was mind blowing.

As well as finding in favour of most of my complaints, the Ombudsman also expressed what she described as 'grave concerns' about the practices of some police officers. These included:

— failing to arrest informants for crimes they had allegedly confessed to;
— hiding intelligence that on several occasions informants were involved in murder and other serious crime;
— arresting informants and performing lengthy sham interviews and then releasing them without charge;
— creating deliberately misleading interview notes;
— failing to record and maintain original interview notes and failing to record notes of meetings with informants;
— failing to record in investigation papers that an informant was a suspect even though he was arrested for that crime;
— failing to tell the Director of Public Prosecutions that an informant was a suspect in a crime in a file already before the director;
— withholding intelligence and the names of alleged suspects from police colleagues which could have been used to prevent and detect crime;
— blocking the searches of an informant's home and other locations including a UVF arms dump;
— protecting an informant;
— providing four misleading and inaccurate documents for a court in relation to four separate incidents and cases

where the documents had the effect of protecting an informant;

— finding munitions at an informant's home and doing nothing about it;

— withholding information about the whereabouts of suspects who had fled after a murder;

— giving instruction to junior officers that records should not be completed and there should be no record of the incident;

— no record was kept of a UVF informant having explosives which were used in a crime;

— cancelling 'wanted' status on murder suspects claiming a 'lack of resources';

— destroying or losing forensic exhibits such as metal bars;

— continuing to use informants who were known or suspected of being involved in serious crime;

— failing to comply with UK Home Office guidelines on the use and handling of informants or the Regulation of Investigatory Powers Act (RIPA) when it came into force in 2000.

It was an unbelievable catalogue of failings, blunders, cover-up and — what I had been saying all along — collusion. True, the RUC did arrest some people in connection with Raymond's murder, but the delay in doing so was a disgrace. There was police documentation received in the hours and days after Raymond's murder which indicated that he died following instructions from Mark Haddock, Informant 1 as Mrs O'Loan referred to him. As well as that, other information provided to both CID and Special Branch detectives corroborates this. One of the main suspects in the murder, Willie Young, who had been in prison at the time of the murder and was on weekend parole from the Maze

Prison when the murder took place, had been named as a suspect two days after the killing. On 14 November the police received further information that Willie Young was involved in the murder, yet he was not arrested until 19 November, a further five days later. What I have always wanted to know is who decided to wait until ten days after the murder to arrest Willie Young? Nobody has ever been able to tell me who in their wisdom made that decision. I think it was a hugely costly mistake as forensic evidence that might have been gathered at an early stage of the investigation had been lost, possibly for ever. I wonder how those detectives would have felt had that happened to a son of theirs.

Reading the report, I was struck by the number of disturbing facts Mrs O'Loan and her team had uncovered not only about the investigation into Raymond's murder, but also how often the police turned a blind eye to Haddock's activities. It didn't matter what he did — beatings, shootings, hijacking, drug dealing, extortion — the Special Branch gave him a free run because in their eyes he was of more use to them on the street than behind bars. Even when he had confessed to murder, the most serious offence, the Special Branch still didn't bring him to heel and put him behind bars where he deserved to be. No decent, rational person could explain why Haddock was allowed to continue to work as a police informant when the police knew he was up to his neck in serious crime. And to add insult to injury, the police were actually paying him tens of thousands of pounds of taxpayers' money. It was like they had their own hired hit-man on their books.

I had taken in as much information as I could and everything appeared to be in place. I headed home to freshen up before the press conference. I closed my bomb-proof wooden front door, sat down on the sofa and thought of what I had been told just a short while earlier. Everything that had happened over the past nine years was going through my head, from the day the police told me of Raymond's murder until the present day. In the privacy of my home, I shed a tear for my son. My tears were tears of regret. One of my biggest regrets was that I had never put my arms around Raymond and told him how much I loved him. It was that macho thing in me that would not let me express my true feelings. It is silly, really. For a couple of hours I was on my own until the police arrived to take me to the press conference. They had been organised by Mrs O'Loan, and fair play to her for making sure I arrived safely. I jumped into the back of the police car and off we roared to east Belfast to the hotel. When we arrived, the car park was packed with large satellite trucks, television crews, photographers and reporters. Mrs O'Loan's press officer Tim Gracey had told me there was a great deal of interest in the report, but I was genuinely surprised and pleased that the press had come out in such numbers to inform the public what Mrs O'Loan had found out from her exhaustive enquiries. A woman who had never known Raymond was about to tell the truth to the world.

The day my family and I had waited for for so long had finally arrived. The adrenalin was pumping again through my veins along with the morphine injection. One of the two would get me through the day.

11.
At Last I am Finally Vindicated

I walked up the steep hill to the entrance of the four-star Stormont Hotel with my black two-piece suit over my shoulder in a suit carrier. Justice for Raymond was another step closer, but the organisation that had killed him was still intent on trying to kill me.

Twice that day uniformed police had called to my house to hand me official PSNI warnings that attacks were being planned against me. Did the UVF think I was like them, cowards? They should have known by this time, nine years after Raymond's murder, that they could not scare me. It showed that the UVF were worried and they were about to be seen for what they were, terrorists controlled and financed by the State.

Following a few yards behind me were members of my family. Vivienne was there along with my two sons, Gareth and Glenn. The day before we all appeared for the first time together in the *Sunday World*, united as a family for young Raymond. It was the first time ever that Vivienne had been photographed in this context; it was also the first time she had been interviewed. It was not because she did not want to talk about her son being murdered, or about how much she missed him, and what she thought of those who had killed him. However, even though we were separated, I had protected her from the press and she was happy for me to do the talking for our family. Young Raymond's murder had greatly affected her health. She was no different from any mother who has lost a son. I knew it had broken her heart and she never got over his vicious death. She had lost her son and was not able to say goodbye to him properly. How cruel is that? How cruel is it to disfigure a person so badly that his parents can't kiss him on the cheek, stroke his hair one last time or make sure he was as neatly and tidily dressed as they would want him to be? Any mother in that situation would have suffered just like Vivienne did, and I have often wished I could have changed that, that I could have mended her broken heart had I been there to save our son.

It was around 10 a.m. and it was just an hour or so before Mrs O'Loan would tell the world that the RUC Special Branch had colluded in my son's murder. Moments earlier as the police car swept into the hotel driveway, I looked out of the rear window and noticed a group of protesters gathered, some of them carrying placards regarding State collusion. No doubt some of them were victims as well, but what I didn't want was a political protest. This was not a political matter. Rather it was a question of justice.

The problem in Northern Ireland has been that you always have people in both the nationalist and unionist communities who are more interested in political point-scoring than seeking justice. Some of those hypocrites don't give a damn about justice. To some, the fact that the victims belonged to the opposite side seemed to justify some of the killings in their warped minds. As far as I was concerned, if you are going to protest about State-sponsored murders, then you have to protest about all paramilitary murders. Murder is murder. One murder is no less horrendous than another. One parent's pain is no less or more than another's. Thankfully the protesters stayed outside the hotel and did not attempt to take their protest inside.

I was met at the door by a number of television crews, photographers and reporters who wanted to know how I felt. I can't remember exactly what I said, but it was along the lines that Mrs O'Loan would confirm everything I had been saying for years: that a police informant ordered my son's murder and that the RUC protected him from prosecution on many, many occasions. I said I had been dismissed as a crank by the police and was being fobbed off as if I meant nothing, and that my son's death meant nothing. But I was not being passed off any more and Mrs O'Loan would see to that. Inside the hotel we were given a private room where my family and friends, who had turned up to give us moral support, enjoyed a cup of tea, sandwiches and biscuits. It helped relax us, steady our nerves. Also mingling around in the hotel foyer and the large conference room were several political figures. What struck me was they were the political leaders of the main Nationalist and Republican parties; I saw no one from the Unionist parties. Yet again the Unionist leaders were ignoring Raymond's murder and the Ombudsman's report. I wondered had 'they' something to be frightened about.

When we entered the conference room it was packed with the media and large spotlights lit up the stage where Mrs O'Loan was about to make her address. I walked in with my son Gareth with our heads held high and took our seats on the left. Glenn was looking after his mother. Up until Sunday, 21 January, Vivienne had kept a low profile. If there was going to be any danger, it was going to be directed at me, not her.

She had suffered enough and I had watched her many times crying over Raymond. But that morning in the Stormont Hotel I honestly believed Raymond was looking down on his mum to give her the strength and support to get through the day. He would have been proud of the dignified way she conducted herself that day. I know I was.

Mrs O'Loan's words reverberated around the room. I sat in total disbelief at just how much Nuala's team had uncovered — corruption, collusion, cover-ups and murders. The list just went on and on. At times I had to close my eyes as I felt so emotional listening to her. She pulled no punches and didn't spare anyone. This is what she told the world's press that day:

Operation Ballast analysed a small part of the informant handling of Special Branch RUC/PSNI. The investigation examined the activities of a number of Special Branch officers of all ranks to Informant 1, and also the other informants who were associated with him. There is no reason to believe that the findings of this investigation are isolated. Indeed given that many of the failings identified in the course of the investigation were systemic, this is highly likely and the implications of this are very serious.

In the course of this investigation it has emerged that all of the informants at the centre of this investigation were members of the UVF. There was no effective management of these informants, and as a consequence of the practices of Special Branch, the position of the UVF particularly in north Belfast and Newtownabbey was consolidated and strengthened.

The handling of informants by Detective Sergeant M and Detective Constable A was not satisfactory.

There was no management intervention to ensure that informants were registered properly and no review of the officers' performance as handlers. PSNI have provided no evidence that any action was taken by the RUC to deal with this.

There is evidence that information was withheld by handlers. Instructions were given that matters should not be recorded.

A culture of subservience to Special Branch developed within the RUC. Officers in the rest of the RUC have articulated quite clearly that Special Branch maintained control over those normal ethical policing activities which might affect either Special Branch informants or Special Branch operations. The consequence of this was that, in the absence of effective Chief Officer management of Special Branch, it acquired domination over the rest of the organisation which inhibited some normal policing activities.

The effect of that dysfunction was that, whilst undoubtedly Special Branch officers were effective in preventing bombing, shootings and other attacks, some informants were able to continue to engage in terrorist activities including murders without the Criminal Investigation Department having the ability to deal with them for some of those offences.

On occasions this also resulted in crimes being permitted by informants with the prior knowledge of Special Branch officers. Informants engaged in such crimes were not subject to any of the controls inherent in the system for the use of Participating Informants devised by the Home Office for use by all police forces. On occasion, despite the fact that they had not given informants Participating Informant status, police nevertheless watched as serious terrorist crimes were committed by their informants.

The Police Ombudsman was concerned also at the attitude of some Special Branch and CID officers to their obligations as police officers. Some officers have articulated the belief that they had no function beyond intelligence gathering. Successive Police Acts have provided that the primary duties of a police officer are to protect life and property, and to prevent and detect crime.

Whilst acting as an informant, and with the knowledge of some Special Branch and CID officers, informants moved through the ranks of the UVF to senior positions. The evidence clearly shows that Informant 1's behaviour, including alleged murder, was not challenged by Special Branch, and those who sought to bring him to justice were blocked repeatedly. Records were minimised, exaggerated, fabricated and must also have been destroyed. Informant 1 would have been well aware of the level of protection which he was afforded.

Whilst Informant 1 was involved in drug dealing, he was not only protected by Special Branch but he was also given huge sums of public money in return for such services as he provided. Indeed on one occasion he is recorded as having provided information which led police to stop a car containing him and two other leading UVF men, all of whom were police informants. No arrests followed yet Informant 1 was paid £3,000.

This investigation demonstrates graphically the dangers of a separated and effectively unaccountable specialist intelligence department with extensive and largely uncontrolled powers. No effective analysis could have been made by the RUC/PSNI over the years of the implications of the totality of the information about, and activities of, the informants who have been identified during this investigation.

In many other crimes described in this report there were witnesses, who drew either police attention to a crime or volunteered to give evidence, some of it quite specific. There was also one occasion in which the victim of a punishment shooting gave extensive information to the police about what had happened to him. In all these situations the individuals involved were either seeking to assist the police or to be protected by the police. The Police Ombudsman has found that on a number of occasions the police did not use these opportunities to further their investigations. This had two consequences: firstly the investigation did not proceed, and secondly failure by police to use evidence tendered by witnesses to paramilitary shootings and other activity must have given rise to a lack of confidence among the people that there was any point in assisting the police when such crimes were committed. The consequence of this would inevitably have been that the police became less effective and community confidence in policing was reduced.

This investigation demonstrates that one of the greatest dangers to any anti-terrorist work is that, if those charged with intelligence gathering and investigation do not abide by the rules, and if those who manage them do not operate effectively to ensure compliance with both law and policy, the risk of terrorist attacks is enhanced, not reduced.

It remains the case that there are many officers in the RUC/PSNI who served bravely and honourably, some even making the ultimate sacrifice. On many occasions in the course of the work of the office, the Police Ombudsman has identified examples of excellent policing. This is in stark contrast to the activities and systemic failures identified in this report.

I was totally disgusted by what Mrs O'Loan had found. It was incredible that a police force charged with protecting life was more interested in protecting murdering, drug-dealing informants. How could the Special Branch withhold intelligence relating to specific murders from CID detectives? There was only one reason and that was to protect the likes of Mark Haddock and other informants in north Belfast and Newtownabbey.

Mrs O'Loan also told us how she defined the term 'collusion'. Many believed that the word referred to police handing over guns and pictures of targets and telling their informants to go and shoot them. It is not as black and white as that. Mrs O'Loan said she followed the definitions of collusion as set out by Lord Stevens and retired Canadian Judge Peter Cory. Stevens was the former commissioner to the Metropolitan Police in London who conducted three separate investigations into collusion between the security forces and loyalist paramilitaries since 1989. He defined collusion as 'the wilful failure to keep records, the absence of accountability, the withholding of intelligence and records, the extreme of agents being involved in murder'. Cory, who conducted inquiries into the murders of Pat Finucane, Robert Hamill, Rosemary Nelson and Billy Wright, said: 'The definition of collusion must be reasonably broad. That is to say that army and police forces must not act collusively by ignoring or turning a blind eye to the wrongful acts of their servants or agents, or supplying information to assist them in their wrongful acts, or encouraging them to commit wrongful acts. Any lesser definition would have the effect of condoning or even encouraging State involvement in crimes thereby shattering all public confidence in these important agencies.'

It was not hard to come to the opinion that the RUC/PSNI colluded not only with Mark Haddock but with many other informants as well. As I sat listening to her statement, I knew I was right to have pursued these UVF killers and expose their dirty dealings with the Special Branch. With every word I felt totally vindicated in my campaign for justice and the truth. In fact, I felt more than vindicated. The extent of the Ombudsman's findings was more than I could ever have expected after walking into her office in May 2002. Sure I felt like jumping up and shouting, 'I told you so.' But there was no need to, as the country and the world were listening to a brave and stubborn woman, appointed by the government to investigate alleged police wrongdoing. Nuala O'Loan was her own person in every way, and the security forces were living to regret it. Never in my wildest dreams did I believe she and her team would expose such rotten apples at the heart of a police force which only a few years earlier had been given the highest award from the Queen for gallantry, the George Cross. I wonder what she thought of them that day watching the news live on Sky. The force to whom she had given such a distinguished award had colluded in murder.

I was grateful to all those who had tried to help my family: Gerry Adams, Lady Sylvia Hermon, Bertie Ahern, Pat Rabbitte, Jane Winters from the British Irish Rights Watch, Darwin Templeton, the SDLP leader Mark Durkan, one of the most decent politicians I met, Naomi Long from the Alliance Party, my old friend Mark Langhammer, my mate Frank McNeill, a true gentleman, and many, many more, the majority of whom I had never met before, all holding different political views yet all prepared to help us achieve our objective. None of them had doubted me and they were always ready to give advice and help. Going up the Falls Road to meet Gerry Adams was indeed an experience for me, but the welcome he gave me made me feel completely at ease. Some of those who helped were at the press conference; some weren't able to be there. I am sure they were all taken aback by what they heard.

Unionist politicians made the point that republicans would be rubbing their hands with satisfaction, instead of being at the press conference and looking at the faces of Raymond's mother and his two brothers as they listened to actual facts and proof that there was collusion not only in Raymond's murder but in many other murders as well. This was nothing to rub your hands over. It was a disgrace and nothing to be proud of. Raymond would be 32 years old now and probably married with kids. Yet because of a system that allowed police officers to work outside the law, our son had missed out on so much. I wonder how those same police officers feel today and do they ask themselves did they live up to the oath they took when they joined the RUC.

To counteract any criticism of myself and the report, this is what Mrs O'Loan's investigators found in relation to my complaint: 'The Ombudsman has found failures in the investigation of Mr McCord's son. These failures may have subsequently reduced the possibility of anyone being prosecuted for murder.' It also substantiated my complaint that the RUC failed to keep me informed on the progress of my son's murder investigation. But what investigation? I have to ask. There was no proper investigation. There was no will to prosecute and the Special Branch made sure the killers were not prosecuted. But the sentence that will stick in my mind is this: 'There is no reason to believe the findings of this investigation are isolated.' It was clear to me from this statement that the Special Branch were probably doing the same elsewhere in Belfast and probably in other parts of Northern Ireland. They appeared to be a law unto themselves. They concealed intelligence; they destroyed evidence; they did not comply with regulations governing the use of informants; they failed to keep proper records; and they allowed informants to continue their terrorist activities. These are not my words or those of a policeman with a grudge; these are the words of the Police Ombudsman for Northern Ireland and what she and her team of experienced investigators had discovered.

The words of one officer questioned during the course of Operation Ballast are both revealing and alarming. Detective Sergeant M was questioned about why he didn't arrest Mark Haddock when he had confessed to him that he had been the second gunman in a murder the previous day. His reply was astonishing. He said he did not consider it to be appropriate and that he would not have been permitted to arrest Haddock. He added that in his own view the fact that Haddock had admitted his role in the murder did not amount to an admission, adding that in his opinion it was quite simply intelligence only. M was adamant that he would have arrested Haddock if he had had the authority to do so. Maybe I have missed the point, but I thought every officer had the power of arrest. I have watched countless TV programmes when ordinary constables in England have arrested suspected criminals. It beggars belief that a detective sergeant in the CID could say that, knowing how ludicrous it sounded. A detective sergeant wants us to believe that when a killer like Haddock confesses to murder, he has no authority to arrest him. When then can he arrest killers?

In a television documentary on UTV, *Insight*, a few years ago, Detective Sergeant Johnston Brown (JB), who served for thirty years in the RUC, told reporter Chris Moore (CM):

JB: If you're asking me are there people who had committed murder but got away with it because they were informants, yes, they did. If you're asking me if, on some occasions, the informants went outside those parameters, yes, they did.

CM: Including murder?

JB: Yes, they did. Were they protected by the highest authority? Yes, they were. Could we have put the majority of them in jail in 1997, 1998, 1999? Absolutely. Would lives have been saved time and time again? Yes, indeed. There appeared to be no will to prosecute certain individuals. I couldn't understand it and I spoke of my reservations, but you're a voice in the wilderness.

These are the words of a seasoned detective who operated for many years in the RUC's CID murder detective squad in north Belfast. This is the same detective who helped to put away Johnny Adair for directing UFF terrorism. The words from that interview which jumped out at me were that certain individuals were being protected by the highest authority and there was no will to prosecute them. Here we had a police detective sergeant supporting what Irish Labour leader Pat Rabbitte had told the Dáil. Yet these two men had never met, didn't know each other, came from different countries, backgrounds and political views but were in absolute agreement with each other. When I watched and listened to Johnston Brown that night on television saying that killers were being protected, I thought that surely someone at the highest level had to be held responsible for letting killers get away with murder. I thought at that moment that it was time for an end to political point-scoring and instead seek truth and justice. How much more convincing did the Unionist politicians need than the words of a servant of the Crown that collusion was not just confined to republicans but was happening within the Protestant community.

Mrs O'Loan also found that the RUC and PSNI had failed to keep me informed of the progress of the investigation into Raymond's murder. But again, what investigation? The police were running the killers as informants and it wouldn't have taken a great deal of detective work to put them behind bars. My son had just become another statistic to them, another casualty.

But the investigation into my son's murder is no different from those carried out in the years before. In 1991 Mark Haddock admitted to the police that he was involved in an attempt to murder a man just days before. He admitted this to both his Special Branch and CID handlers, yet he was never charged. The RUC already knew about his involvement before his confession because an undercover surveillance unit watched as Haddock took over a house and the owner's car was stolen and used in the sectarian murder bid. The following year he was involved in another attempted murder and was arrested and released without charge. The Ombudsman's report was scathing of the RUC. The findings stated: 'The information was mishandled in the first instance, and then destroyed or suppressed thus protecting Haddock from potential prosecution.'

But the protection of Mark Haddock from being charged with my son's murder is not an isolated case. Mrs O'Loan's team also found there was collusion inside the RUC between the Special Branch and the CID not to charge Haddock with the murder of 'Good Samaritan' Sharon McKenna in January 1993. How do you describe a police force that covers up murders? To this day, even though Haddock is the main suspect in the murder, 'he has not been properly investigated for it', the report found. And that is in spite of the fact that he confessed to killing her on three separate meetings with his handlers and not once was he arrested for such a heinous sectarian murder of a young woman who was helping a Protestant neighbour.

In the course of her inquiry Mrs O'Loan received four different versions of conversations Haddock had with his CID and Special Branch handlers about Ms McKenna's murder. When he was eventually arrested, nine days after the murder on 26 January, he was interviewed a total of 37 times, 19 by his CID handler, Detective Constable A. These interviews were conducted in the presence of Detective Sergeant GG, who told Mrs O'Loan he felt like 'he was going through the motions' during the interrogation and he believed Haddock was not going to say anything of importance about Ms McKenna's murder. In the words of Mrs O'Loan, 'these were sham interviews'. But what is even more astonishing is that in the weeks following the murder Haddock's payments from the Special Branch increased from £100 a month to £160 a month, even though he was the chief suspect in the killing. His Special Branch handler said this was because of the intelligence he had provided about the murder of Ms McKenna. In effect, he was getting paid from the public purse to give information about his own involvement in a murder. The Special Branch even gave him money to go on a holiday to Spain until the heat died down after the McKenna murder. To me, that is just a licence to murder.

There was also evidence of collusion found in the murder of Sean McParland, who was shot dead while babysitting his four grandchildren at his daughter's house in Skegoneil, north Belfast, on 25 February 1994. The man who fired the fatal shots was the future brigadier of south east Antrim UVF, Gary 'The Beast' Haggarty, another registered Special Branch informant. Mark Haddock and two other UVF men were also identified as being involved in the killing and all four were arrested. But from Mrs O'Loan's report, the police were 'just going through the motions' as well in this case. Was anyone charged with Mr McParland's murder? No. Were Haddock and Haggarty removed as registered informants? No. The report on Mr McParland's murder concludes: 'This was indicative of collusion.'

Three months later, on 18 May 1994, Gary Convie and Eamon Fox were shot dead while eating their lunch in a car at a construction site in the loyalist Tigers Bay area of north Belfast. Haddock and another informant were seen in the area prior to the shooting and they were later arrested along with a number of others. While being held at Castlereagh Holding Centre, Haddock asked for a razor and was given one. At the time of the murder, witnesses had reported to the police that the gunman who killed Mr Convie and Mr Fox was wearing a goatee beard. However, when Haddock was photographed in custody the day after the murder, his goatee beard had been removed. I find it astonishing that the police would allow him to change his physical appearance in custody before any identification parade could take place. As Mrs O'Loan discovered, the police didn't even bother to hold an identification parade. It would have been pointless anyway, given that the police had allowed him to change his looks. Was Haddock charged with murder? No. Did the police cancel his employment as an informant even though he was identified as the gunman? No. Sadly, this was more evidence of RUC collusion with a UVF killer and a well-paid informant.

These are only a few examples of RUC collusion within a small area of north Belfast, where a UVF gang were free to target and kill. But it didn't stop there. Mrs O'Loan's team found that police officers had created interview notes which were deliberately misleading; that they failed to record and maintain original interview notes; and on many occasions failed to keep notes of meetings with informants. Then there were the lengthy 'sham' interviews where informants were not even challenged about their involvement in murders, only for them to be released to kill again. It was like they were hauled in off the street for a cosy chat over a cup of tea to give the impression within their own organisation that they were in trouble. But nothing could have been further from the truth. It is exasperating to think that police officers would deliberately conceal the vital intelligence from CID colleagues that up to 'three informants' had been involved in a murder and other serious crimes. Similarly at least four misleading and inaccurate documents were prepared for possible consideration by the court and these documents had the desired effect of protecting an informant from conviction. Another example was the police finding guns at an informant's house and doing absolutely nothing about it. The result was no charges were preferred and the killer was free to walk the streets again. Then there were officers who knew where murder suspects had fled to after a murder and withheld that vital information from the investigating CID officers. Some officers failed to keep official records linking a UVF informant to the possession of explosives; while others told junior Special Branch officers not to complete records on serious terrorist crimes.

In 2003 the Police Surveillance Commissioner carried out an inspection of the handling of Mark Haddock by the Special Branch. The commissioner found serious failings by the Special Branch in complying with the requirements of the law in relation to the handling of informants, 'covert human intelligence sources' (CHIS). His report on Haddock stated: 'This CHIS is a high risk source and the management process has not been documented to the standard required. There is a failure to document regular reviews taking into consideration the position of the CHIS in a terrorist organisation and the criminal intelligence regarding his own conduct. There has been a failure to ensure that the use and conduct of this source has been considered at Chief Officer level. There has been a failure to secure and preserve original material from contacts or meetings between handlers and the source. There has been a failure to follow the Association of Chief Police Officers/Her Majesty's Customs & Excise Manual of Minimum Standards in relation to CHIS. . . .' This was not locker room gossip in relation to how the police ran informants as some Unionist politicians would have the public believe. Nor was it locker room gossip that the Special Branch suppressed intelligence on a UVF bomb attack on the Sinn Féin office in Monaghan. The Special Branch even handed the bomb to the UVF informants who included Haddock.

As well as the murders, drug dealing was a major problem in north Belfast. Haddock and his motley crew, many of whom were also paid police informants, were living off the profits of dealing in death. Information was coming to the RUC of his involvement in drug dealing, but the Drugs Squad appeared to turn a blind eye to this. They claimed they didn't have the manpower to deal with it and in reality were more concerned with the 'big fish' further up the chain of supply.

Were they trying to tell me that it was all right to sell drugs as long as you were not a major supplier? Apparently if you were an informant, especially if you were on the Special Branch payroll, you were safe from the police to sell drugs.

These facts are only the tip of a very large iceberg called collusion. Even throughout the ten years I was shouting from the rooftops about RUC collusion with the UVF in north Belfast, I never dreamt just how rotten and corrupt parts of the police force were. No one would have believed that in a free, democratic society the forces of law and order would be complicit in such serious crimes. Who would believe that the police would hand back a bomb to terrorists to be used in an attack? Today when we hear and read in the media about the worldwide threat to peace and stability from Islamic terrorists, we have to ask ourselves why the police in Northern Ireland acted in such a criminal way. I urge people not to heed the words of certain politicians and police officers when they talk about the 'lives that were saved'. How many times have they trotted out that line all through the Troubles? How would they feel if it was their son or daughter lying on a mortuary slab or in a closed coffin, knowing that the killer was an informant and that the police had the intelligence to put him away but refused to share it with the detectives conducting a murder inquiry? There was one law for the CID and one law for the Special Branch.

In 1997, the year my son was murdered, the police actually ignored their own document called 'The Management and Use of Informants'. A decision was taken by chief officers that it would not apply to the use of Special Branch informants. In essence, Special Branch informants were now being elevated to operate above and beyond the law by the same officers who were paid to uphold it. Drug dealing, murder, attempted murder, shootings, beatings, it made no difference to the tout-ridden Mount Vernon UVF. They all knew they were safe from prosecution as the shadowy hand of the Special Branch made sure of that. One informant was touting on another informant. From the outside it looked like a vicious circle of tit-for-tat touting, where one informant was played off against another to find out what was really going on in certain areas. But there was no product at the end of all this intelligence because no one was being charged and convicted. To me it was a pointless waste of public money and police resources, and innocent members of the public paid the ultimate price — they were murdered — for the petty jealousies and games played within the corridors of police stations.

In May 2002, when I entered the Police Ombudsman's building in Belfast, the UVF could not know just how it would turn out. They believed that just over four and a half years after Raymond's murder the public and the media would be fed up listening to me. But they would have been justified in that belief, given the number of murders the organisation had carried out and apparently got away with. Their problem was they had never come up against such a determined family before, one that would repeatedly refuse to lie down under the barrage of threats. No Unionist politician was jumping up and shouting about the UVF killing people in the unionist community despite the fact that they had declared a ceasefire in October 1994. It was easy for the UVF to get away with it because as they were killing their own Protestants, people believed they would not have killed these people without good reason. But this was a killing machine out of control which, at the time the ceasefire was called, had started to enjoy the act of murder. The more sadistic, the more brutal, the more they enjoyed it.

I was an intended victim of that murder machine many

times. The UVF leadership based on the Shankill Road actively encouraged their north Belfast brigade, in particular 3rd battalion Mount Vernon, to kill me. This was to have been their easy option as they did not want to deal with Haddock who was making too much money for the organisation. He was a one-man, money-making machine for the UVF and the more he gave them, the more they protected him. Haddock was not only protected by his Special Branch handlers but also by his two superior officers, his 'drunken' brigadier Rab Warnock and the UVF's chief of staff John 'Bunter' Graham, who were both highly paid Special Branch informants and who were never going to give an order to kill him.

For a start, the Special Branch would not have allowed it as he was one of their prized intelligence assets in north Belfast. You don't shoot the goose that is laying the golden eggs. My battle against Haddock was a two-horse race and Warnock and Graham backed the wrong horse. If the Special Branch had dealt with Haddock back in 1997, my son's murder would not have become a recurring nightmare for them. But I now know that they would not have given the clearance to kill Haddock and many of the UVF men on the Shankill Road know that the leadership is run by the hidden hand of the security forces. How has the chief of staff lasted so long? How come he has never discovered any touts in the UVF? I know they can't speak out because to do so would result in a bullet to the back of the head. To them I say: Don't worry. I haven't finished yet. I brought down the UVF in Mount Vernon along with serial killer Haddock, and I intend to bring a few more down as well. My fight goes on until such time as the UVF hands over to the PSNI my son's killers or the killers are arrested and jailed. But until then I will continue to expose and unnerve those UVF killers right up to the day they stand in a court of law.

You always proclaim 'No surrender', yet your leader Bunter Graham surrendered to the police many years ago for his thirty pieces of silver and a cosy life betraying his so-called 'comrades'. How does that square with his war cry of 'For God and Ulster'? Maybe Graham could explain to his men what it means and who is the 'God' in his community. As far as I know, though I am not a church-going parent, God does not condone murder. In fact he said it was wrong to take another person's life. You don't have to be a Christian to know that life is a precious gift and everyone has the right to life. My son had the right to life; so had Sharon McKenna, Eamon Fox, Gary Convie, Sean McParland, Peter McTasney, John Harbinson — the list of UVF victims in north Belfast goes on.

What started out as a search for truth and justice for young Raymond has also helped to enlighten the families of these other victims as to what happened to their loved ones and how their lives could have, and should have, been saved. I can say with hand on heart that I have been vindicated in the eyes of the people of Northern Ireland and that has meant a lot to me and my family. It has been a long journey. Many times I was dismissed as a crank by those who promoted a sinister propaganda campaign against me. These same people labelled me an aggrieved father looking for sympathy or a 'media junkie'. All I am is the father of a lovely son who was brutally murdered on the orders of an agent of the State and I wasn't going to take no for an answer. I was brought up to believe that the truth will always come out and I believe the Police Ombudsman got right to the heart of the truth. My fight goes on.

12.
From Agent Helen to Agent Roxy

There are only a few people in this world I can honestly say I hate, and of those Mark Haddock is top of the tree. The sound of his name makes my blood boil and I am filled with a rage that is hard to explain. He epitomises everything that is corrupt in a person and he has robbed many people of loved ones, brothers, sisters, sons and daughters. How he sleeps in his prison bed is beyond me. He is a killer who has no remorse. For nine years I complained to policemen, held top level meetings with politicians of all persuasions and with the help of the media, the support of my family and a close circle of friends, I finally succeeded in my campaign to expose Haddock for what he was, a killer, a drug dealer, an extortionist, a wealthy criminal and a paid RUC Special Branch agent who was given *carte blanche* to murder people without even a whiff of the law breathing down his neck. It was as if the security forces had their own hired gun at their disposal, someone who could drive into Protestant and Catholic areas, go in someone's front door, shoot them dead as they stood in their homes and just walk away.

Monday, 22 January 2007, will go down in history as the

day the explosive Police Ombudsman's report into my son's murder rocked the British establishment to its core, sent policemen scurrying to their lawyers for legal advice and lifted the lid on how the RUC Special Branch and an illegal paramilitary organisation, the UVF, colluded in murder after murder. Since that day the whole world, and everyone else who was prepared to listen, has been given the full facts of what went on inside the UVF in north Belfast and south-east Antrim. The report showed exactly what Haddock had been doing for twelve years while in the care and pay of both the CID and the Special Branch as one of their so-called prized informants. It was hard for some Unionist politicians to swallow the truth when they came out with statements like, 'How many lives did he save?' You would have thought listening to them that the victims of his heinous crimes didn't matter. These same politicians also trotted out the line about the 'bigger picture'. I can understand critics of the report, in particular Unionist politicians and police officers, either still serving or retired, showing loyalty to the RUC/PSNI, but I ask, at what price? Does the price come down to ignoring the fact that Haddock seemed to control the Special Branch with his actions and as a result was able to do what he liked, when he liked, and without fear of repercussions. I don't know of anyone who can admit to murder within twenty-four hours of shooting dead an innocent young Catholic woman, Sharon McKenna, and not be charged. But as I have found during nearly ten years of investigations, this was par for the course for Haddock due to the Special Branch.

Detective Constable Trevor McIlwrath of the RUC's Belfast Regional Criminal Investigation Department (CID) recruited Mark Haddock as an informant while he was in his teens. McIlwrath gave Haddock the codename, Agent Helen, after his girlfriend and doctor's receptionist Helen McAllister, the daughter of former UVF life sentence prisoner Billy McAllister. During his first few years he supplied McIlwrath with information about those involved in criminality in the Mount Vernon area. Even though Haddock himself was involved in petty crime and arson, the police viewed him as someone they could control whilst working for them. But where did it all go wrong for Haddock? I don't know the answer to that question, but what I do know is that as the Troubles showed no sign of ending, Haddock joined the ranks of the UVF's 3rd battalion of Mount Vernon and Shore Road. Even though he was a CID informant, the CID saw no harm in him joining a proscribed organisation such as the UVF. In his early days as a low level informant inside the UVF, he was to gather information on members of that organisation and their movements. Any 'loose talk' he picked up from conversations at parties or in pubs would then be passed on to his handlers. At this stage in the late 1980s, Haddock was not involved in the UVF murder campaign of targeting mainly Catholics, but that was to change in the years to come when he would be leading the onslaught from the front. To his credit, McIlwrath seemed to be in control of Haddock and kept a tight rein on his activities, that is until 1991.

After several years of being controlled by the CID as an informant, the time came when the Special Branch wanted an input into Haddock's role. In fact Haddock was to be jointly run between the Special Branch and the CID. But because Haddock was a member of a proscribed organisation, police rules stated that the Special Branch would take the lead role in running Haddock as it had primacy in Northern Ireland in gathering intelligence on all paramilitary organisations. Now that he was on the Special

Branch payroll with the code, Agent 20/1240, Haddock could expect a bumper return on his information. As a result he was to be paid a monthly retainer plus bonuses or incentives. On one occasion Haddock was paid a whopping £10,000, yet nobody can explain why he received such an enormous amount of taxpayers' money. He also received £1,000 in cash as a 'welfare' payment as he needed some work carried out. When his handlers were asked if they had verified his claim as to why he needed the money, amazingly they replied that no checks had been carried out. A breakdown was made of payments Haddock received that could be traced. He received retainers to the tune of £34,140, incentive payments of £42,000, operational payments of £1,700, and 'welfare' payments totalling £2,000 — not bad for a man who was suspected of being involved in some shape or form in up to sixteen murders. None of this is fiction or made up, as critics of the Police Ombudsman's Office would have the public believe. All these facts were uncovered during a protracted and difficult investigation into the murky world of how Haddock was being run by the Special Branch.

But the startling facts uncovered inside the world of smoke and mirrors surrounding the Special Branch do not end there. Mrs O'Loan's investigators also found the following: Haddock was a member of the UVF who progressed up through the ranks of the organisation with the obvious knowledge and approval of the Special Branch; he was never a registered CID informant, yet he provided information to a detective constable and a detective sergeant in the CID; he became a Special Branch informant in 1991 and over the following twelve years was the subject of 500 pieces of intelligence provided by other informants; he was suspected by the RUC/PSNI of being involved in ten murders; he was suspected of being involved in the attempted murder of ten others; he was directly involved in a bomb attack in Co. Monaghan in 1997; he was involved in vicious punishment beatings and shootings, some of which were the most severe meted out by the UVF in Belfast; he was knee deep in the importation and supply of both class A and class B drugs, to such an extent that even the RUC Drugs Squad wanted a piece of him so that he could lead them to dealers further up the supply chain; he was involved in attempting to pervert the course of justice; he was never given 'participating status' as an informant by either the RUC or the PSNI to become actively involved in terrorism or criminal activities; and he was never properly investigated for his involvement in these crimes.

Haddock also had an extensive criminal record dating back to his teens, which included theft, arson, serious assault and criminal damage. During the course of the O'Loan investigation, the Ombudsman's staff found a document from his joint CID/Special Branch file where a detective inspector attached to the Special Branch described him as a 'particularly difficult source to handle who tells only a fraction of what he knows and for this reason would require strong, careful, fully controlled and co-ordinated handling'. Some uniformed and CID officers who worked in north Belfast between 1990 and 2003 knew him as a 'well-known terrorist and criminal' who was involved in racketeering, drug dealing, feuding with the rival UDA and other general crime. Some of those officers said there were rumours circulating in north Belfast that Haddock was an informant and appeared to be a 'protected species' as he was heavily involved in crime but was rarely held to account. Amazingly, given all that was known about him inside the police, the RUC and the PSNI Special Branch paid him a total of around £80,000, yet no one questioned these payments, even though there was an abundance of intelligence from other informants about his nefarious activities.

A year after Sir Hugh Orde was appointed PSNI Chief Constable, Haddock was finally dropped as an informant in 2003 following a complaint from Mrs O'Loan that she believed informants on the police payroll were acting outside the law. The letter from Mrs O'Loan prompted a root and branch review of all informants and some 40 per cent of all those passing information to the police were dropped from the PSNI payroll. I am sure Haddock's role as a criminal, a terrorist and an informant has raised a few eyebrows, but how the hell did the Special Branch continue to run him, given all they knew about him? There has never been a satisfactory answer to this very pertinent question and I am resigned to the fact that there probably never will be.

However, none of the facts above would ever have been revealed if I had kept quiet and not pushed for answers to my son's murder. What I do know now is that between 1991 and 1995 Haddock was run jointly by the CID and the Special Branch, and from 1995 until his demise in 2003 by the Special Branch alone. I would have thought when I started to make noises to the RUC in 1997 about Haddock and how he had ordered young Raymond's murder, coupled with the intelligence provided by other informants, that the Special Branch would have dropped him like a hot potato. Sadly, for me and for other families who were victims of Haddock's work, they didn't, and for reasons known only to themselves. In north Belfast, which had become known throughout the Troubles as 'murder mile', where killers visited homes as regularly as the milkman, Haddock became a feared man. He didn't have a reputation for fighting on his own or using his fists; his reputation was borne out of the fact that he would not hesitate to use guns, hammers, hatchets, baseball bats, iron bars or anything else he could get his blood-soaked hands on that would inflict the most grievous of injuries on his prey. Yet the victims had no recourse to the law, as the law was protecting him from what he deserved, jail. There was no one they could approach, not even the RUC or the PSNI. It is no wonder Haddock did as he liked: the Branch were his great protectors.

Yet anytime the police suspected *me* of breaking the law, they did everything they could to prosecute me. Looking back on these years the RUC/PSNI had put me down as a kind of lone wolf, like a Charles Bronson-style character who fought a one-man campaign against the paramilitaries. In their eyes it appeared to be a better use of police resources to pursue a lone wolf like me rather than bring to book the drug-dealing, murdering paramilitary gangs that stalked our terrified streets. I was accused over the years of beating up paramilitaries, burning their cars and houses, shooting them, and intimidation — all this from one man. I am surprised I ever had time to sleep! If I was guilty of all the things the police accused me of doing, then I am glad I helped the Northern Ireland economy and kept people in work: the policemen who arrested me for questioning; the nurses, doctors and ambulance personnel tending to the injured paramilitaries; the firemen putting out their blazing cars; the taxi drivers who earned a living from ferrying around the paramilitaries because they had no cars; and the housing officers who had to relocate the displaced thugs. Yet the police would have the people of north Belfast and beyond believe that this was all down to me, Raymond McCord, a working-class family man.

After young Raymond's murder the police were convinced I would attack those who had killed my son. The reality was, they were hoping I would do so, so they could take me off the streets and allow the killers to carry on doing whatever they wanted. But I didn't rise to the provocation. One man who helped me stay within the law was Kenny McClinton, a reformed paramilitary. Kenny is known as a Bible thumper, a Christian. Many times he and his wife spoke to me about not resorting to violence. Kenny learned that the hard way by spending many years in jail for murder and he didn't want me following in his footsteps and going down that road. True, there were times I had no choice and had to go outside the law, but that was due to intimidation by the UDA and the UVF. They even formed a pact to kill me. Although I knew my life was in great danger from Haddock and the UVF, I was determined to expose him as an out-of-control informant who was killing at will.

I met several contacts who told me various stories about Haddock. One was that in 1997 while serving a sentence for the UVF attack on the Golden Hind pub in Portadown, Co. Armagh, Haddock contacted Billy Wright, the now dead leader of the breakaway Loyalist Volunteer Force (LVF), and told him he wanted to join his organisation and would bring his men from north Belfast into his ranks to swell his numbers against his old adversaries in the UVF. From what I was told, Wright declined Haddock's request to jump on board. My contacts in the loyalist underworld told me that the consensus among prisoners was that Haddock was a tout. How right they were.

Shortly after Haddock was released from jail, I noticed him a few times loitering in a car near my house. He was always accompanied by young Raymond's so-called mate Darren Moore, or 'Judas' as I call him, who liked to show Haddock his loyalty. On a warm sunny day I was sitting at my mother's front door with a couple of relatives enjoying the sunshine, unaware that danger was lurking around the corner. Haddock and some of his men had seen me drive into my mother's street and they were watching and waiting to see what I was doing. Luckily for me people had spotted them driving around the area before they drove off. But Haddock, Moore and another accomplice didn't go home to their nest in Mount Vernon. Instead they headed to the police station a short distance away and all three made a complaint against me. They alleged that I tried to pull them out of the car at the traffic lights when they turned red. It was absolute nonsense to think that one man would dare to pull three seasoned, tough UVF men from a car, knowing their pedigree as ex-convicts and killers. They tried to convince the RUC that they had to flee for their lives from an unarmed man. Of course the police took their complaint seriously and interviewed me with a view to prosecution, but fortunately for me my relatives confirmed that I never left my mother's front door. We all know that relatives, especially close ones, always tell the truth!

With that matter firmly closed, Haddock was still determined to shut me up as he knew what I knew: that he was a tout. But for all his reputation as the hard man of Mount Vernon, there was no way he would have tried anything against me on his own. He didn't have the guts. He and his mob opted for different tactics against me as the threat of being shot at or attacked didn't scare me. They stooped to a new low when they attacked young Raymond's headstone. On three separate occasions the headstone was smashed, but all this did was make me even more determined to catch up with them. Let me tell you that I know who carried out the desecration of young Raymond's grave and believe me one day those involved will receive a very unwelcome visit from me. It was a promise I made to my son as Gareth, Glenn and I tended to the smashed headstone.

People from all walks of life were disgusted at the desecration, except the UVF who stood idly by and literally did nothing. Nero fiddled while Rome burned. The desecration of a young Protestant's grave on three separate occasions meant nothing to the UVF, the so-called Protestant defenders. Close to where young Raymond is laid to rest are several UVF graves. Never once have I or any member of my family ever dreamt of attacking them in revenge. I believe that no matter what you think of the person lying in the grave, they should be left to rest in peace. Unfortunately the UVF don't think that way.

There was no let-up in the trouble that kept following me in the shape of Haddock and the UVF. I was constantly on my guard looking out for suspicious cars and people generally acting suspiciously. One day as I was driving out of my street in York Road, I spotted a certain UVF man standing at the corner. Within the space of a few minutes I noticed in my rear view mirror Haddock's black BMW on my tail. Inside the flash drug dealer's car were three other men. I knew there was no point in panicking, so I calmly drove along York Road on to Shore Road in the direction of Haddock's Mount Vernon stronghold. I indicated left and took the turn, but Haddock spotted my manoeuvre and drove into another street which ran parallel to the one I was in. At the top of the street I attempted to turn left, but Haddock had me boxed in. I had no choice but to drive straight at them. Haddock wasn't too slow in moving out of the way. As I whizzed past him he shouted threats at me that I was going to die. Mr Big had been reduced to shouting threats against me.

I decided it was time to take Haddock down because at a meeting with my local DUP councillor Nigel Dodds in 1997, the then Chief Constable of the RUC Ronnie Flanagan said to us: 'We never have any evidence against Haddock. If only someone would make a complaint.' I never forgot those words and after Haddock made threats on my life, I drove directly to Newtownabbey Police Station. On arrival I asked for a CID detective, was shown into an interview room and lodged a formal complaint against Haddock that he made a threat to kill me. The chief constable now had what he wanted and I sat back to see how his officers would handle it. Hours later Haddock was arrested. I remember it was a Thursday night and within hours my house, which was just yards from York Road RUC Station, was attacked at the dead of night. Haddock's mob had arrived, which could mean only one thing: I had got his back up. He was in custody and he was trying to intimidate me into withdrawing my complaint against him. For twenty-four hours he was held for questioning and on Friday night he was charged. He was held overnight to appear at a special sitting of Belfast Magistrates Court on Saturday morning. Before he stood in the dock to face the court, charged with making 'threats to kill Mr Raymond McCord', several carloads of UVF men arrived outside my house in Seaview Street revving their engines in an attempt to intimidate me. Not one of them was brave enough to knock at my front door. The police could see what was going on from the CCTV cameras perched high on the security fence around their station, yet as usual no one came to help me. All I had was a hatchet and an Alsatian to defend me from the UVF. I had something else as well: a stomach for a fight, something which Haddock's cronies didn't have. I had had a belly full of Haddock and if they wanted a fight, then I was ready to give them one. I opened the front door and looked out at the UVF men. True to form, they drove away, either to fight the IRA or maybe to change their trousers!

Three weeks after his court appearance, Haddock was a

free man and back on the streets. The DPP in his wisdom had decided on 11 June to drop all the charges against him. The DPP later confirmed to me that this decision was made despite the fact that they had not received a file from the RUC until two months later, on 20 August. How the DPP could make a decision to drop the charges when they hadn't even seen the police file was beyond my understanding. It was utterly astonishing, and I had no doubt that the Special Branch's influence was at work for the DPP to make such a decision. It was the only logical conclusion I could come to.

Haddock might have thought he was untouchable, but I didn't and I wasn't going to let him have any peace. If he and his cronies couldn't let my son rest in peace, then neither would they. I drove into an estate where he was working with a mob of his supporters and then simply drove away. It was my way of telling him that I wasn't finished. Shortly after driving off, I had to stop at the traffic lights at Mount Vernon, when all of a sudden a large Ford Transit van pulled up alongside me. Glaring out from the van was Haddock accompanied of course by a number of his thugs as his back-up. As the van pulled away from the lights, Haddock just smiled at me and I did the same. The van made no attempt to follow me as I headed home. I was only in the house five minutes when the police arrived to tell me that Haddock had made a formal complaint against me, accusing me of pointing a gun at him. I looked at the police in astonishment. Where on God's earth would I get a gun? I'm not a member of the 'People's army', as the UVF liked to call themselves. But it was heartening to see such an immediate response to Haddock's complaint, given that most victims of crime can never get a policeman when they want one. During questioning by the police, I told them that I had no gun, that the complaint was a pack of lies and that Haddock should be charged with wasting police time. The officer looked astounded when I told him what I would have done if I had had a gun and Haddock was sitting in a van beside me. He also knew I was deadly serious when it came to Haddock.

In north Belfast, and in particular in the Protestant areas, Haddock truly believed he was 'king of the castle'. But how wrong he was. His groupies, his hangers-on, were nothing but a waste of space, a bunch of thugs who were to find out some years later that the man they called their boss was a Special Branch puppet. I wonder now how they felt when he was finally exposed, because they must have known for all those years that what I had been saying about him was the truth. Sometimes it is hard for these people to believe the truth, even when it is staring them in the face, but I believe there are many UVF men who believed me from the very start but could not speak out. What Haddock never counted on was that I had no intention of bringing the curtain down on my search for justice and the truth. I just didn't fear him. Would he have liked to meet me on his own up a dark alley one night? No chance. Cowards like him are always found out and he eventually was. If Haddock had fought Trevor Gowdy on his own, he would have been destroyed. I have no doubt about that. But the Mount Vernon UVF were like baying hyenas: it was safer to hunt in a pack than in isolation.

The attempt on Trevor Gowdy's life is just one of a number of unsuccessful attempts by Haddock and his crew to kill people. True, Haddock did save some lives, and that I don't dispute. There was the time in 1991 when he admitted to his Special Branch and CID handlers that he had been involved in an aborted murder attempt in which he and another man hijacked a car. Haddock held the owner and his family hostage while the other drove away to pick up two gunmen. All three men were caught not too far away and the police recovered guns, balaclavas, gloves and a sledgehammer from the car. The three men were charged but Haddock was not, even though undercover police had watched him take over the house. Two of the men were later convicted in relation to that murder bid and also to another sectarian murder in February 1991. One of the guns and bullets was forensically matched to the gun and ammunition used to kill 26-year-old Peter McTasney on the Bawnmore estate. So it is clear that Haddock was the informant who passed on the information that an innocent Catholic was going to be shot dead and the police were able to apprehend the would-be gunmen before they could carry out their dirty deed.

Yes, Haddock saved a life, and in the process had three of his UVF mates arrested and sent to prison with long sentences. But all he was doing was telling the police what he was being paid to do: stop terrorist crimes and help in the arrest of UVF men. However, and unfortunately for many victims and their families, Haddock refused to tell his handlers exactly what he was getting up to. At the same time the police have no excuse for allowing him to continue to work for them, especially after 1993 when he admitted to the murder of the young Catholic woman Sharon McKenna. It has since been established that when he was eventually arrested for that murder, his Special Branch and CID handlers were present at his interviews and were even told by senior police officers to 'babysit' him and make sure he did not admit to murder. What a lovely law enforcement agency the people of Northern Ireland had looking after them! If this were to happen in any other country, the senior police officer would have been before a court on serious charges. But this was Northern Ireland at that time and the Special Branch had its own rules, especially when it came to Haddock.

They had the same rules for the driver of the getaway car

involved in the Sharon McKenna murder. Wheel man Willie Glendinning was also a Special Branch informer. In February 2007 he was removed from Northern Ireland by his police intelligence handlers and his house in Rathcoole emptied of its contents after his cover as an informant inside the UVF had been blown. Since Glendinning was resettled in England, I have spoken to a former sergeant in the Special Branch who told me he left it because he didn't like the way it operated. He told me it was like a competition among Branch officers, who judged how good an informant was by the number of people he was able to kill so that he would be thought of as 'kosher', a person who would definitely not be thought of as working for the Special Branch. It was their way of proving their pedigree to their superiors and it also guaranteed them a speedy rise up the organisation's ranks. Haddock had earned his stripes as a killer, as did the man who fired the fatal shots that killed Sean McParland in 1994, Gary 'The Beast' Haggarty. Like Haddock, he was gaining a reputation in the UVF as a hit-man which also guaranteed him promotion within the organisation's south east Antrim brigade. So here were two known killers and informants who the Special Branch knew were involved in cold-blooded sectarian murders, yet they did nothing to remove them from their books, never mind bring them before a court. That was the extent of the corruption at the highest level inside the Special Branch.

With a number of murders under his belt, the UVF believed it could make Haddock the 'king' of Mount Vernon, where he and his thugs would control it with an iron fist. No one would question him when he became commanding officer of the UVF in the estate. There were many men in Mount Vernon who could have beaten him to pulp in a street fight, but that was never going to happen. I have always wondered how Haddock's mother felt about how the son she brought into the world in 1969 had become such a ruthless, bloodthirsty killer. I have also wondered how she felt when in May 2006 he admitted to her that he had been working for the Special Branch after the UVF shot and seriously injured him. She still lives in Mount Vernon although his step-father Harold has moved out. In return for withdrawing his statements against the two men involved in the shooting, Ronnie 'The Poof' Bowe and Darren 'Judas' Moore, the UVF allowed Haddock's mother to remain in Mount Vernon without fear of any harm coming to her. It wouldn't have painted the UVF in a good light if they had attacked his mother. Throughout his trial for the attempted murder of Trevor Gowdy, Haddock's mother turned up at Belfast Crown Court to hear the evidence, determined to stand by her son.

A decade before the UVF tried to kill Haddock for being a tout, the organisation's leadership asked him to kill Thomas Shepherd who it alleged was a police informant. Haddock was driven to the Towers Tavern pub on the Balee estate in Ballymena on 21 March 1996 by another informant, Terry Fairfield, codenamed Agent Mechanic. After the murder, according to the Ombudsman's report, an informant gave information regarding the murder and named Haddock as one of the gunmen. Subsequent to that another source provided intelligence that Haddock had been in a pub 'spouting about' having shot Thomas Shepherd the year before and gave further information about the murder. But Ombudsman investigators could find no mention of Haddock being named as the gunman, nor was there any record of the intelligence being handed to the CID detectives carrying out the murder inquiry. No one was ever charged in connection with the murder. So in all the murders Haddock was suspected of being involved in, nobody has ever been charged in relation to them. That should not come as any great surprise, for when Haddock brought a large coffee jar bomb to his Special Branch handlers in 1997, his handlers gave it straight back to him so that he and two other informants, John 'Bonzo' Bond and Terry Fairfield, could drive across the border and plant it outside the Sinn Féin office in Monaghan town with no worries about being stopped at security forces checkpoints.

Throughout his years as an informant, Haddock had struck up a close relationship with Terry Fairfield, a Catholic from the New Lodge Road in north Belfast. It was incredible to think that a sectarian killer like Haddock could form such a friendship with a Catholic. Their friendship was so steadfast that when Haddock's girlfriend in Cork, Roxy, had a daughter by him, Fairfield attended the Christening in a Catholic church as the child's godfather. The Special Branch knew about Haddock's relationship with Roxy, an Aer Lingus stewardess, and in 1995 changed his codename to Agent Roxy when it took complete control of him as an informant.

I have often wondered how Terry Fairfield felt about Haddock's direct involvement in the sectarian murders of Catholics, people of his own persuasion and from his own community in north Belfast. He probably doesn't care one little bit. Remember, this is the same man who admitted to his handlers that he supplied the car that was used to carry the gunmen to and from the Heights bar massacre in Loughinisland in June 1994, when six innocent Catholics were shot dead while watching the Republic of Ireland play Italy in the World Cup finals. Three years after the Loughinisland pub massacre, Fairfield was swiftly removed from Northern Ireland by the RUC when the UVF discovered he was an informant and were going to kill him. It was a body blow for Haddock, who had previously told the UVF leadership that he didn't believe Fairfield was a tout. Haddock had been told to protect Fairfield and keep him safe by a detective sergeant in the CID and he was able to do this from his position in the UVF. Fairfield was now a marked man whom the UVF would kill for treason. They didn't have to look too hard for him because Haddock and other UVF informants in north Belfast visited him regularly at his new home in Wales. He had been resettled there by the Special Branch who helped him buy a pub and guesthouse. What a gathering of informants, touts, agents and spies! It reminds me of the Hollywood film, *My Blue Heaven*, in which Steve Martin plays a Mafia hit-man who turns against his own, becomes an informer and is resettled in a town full of informers from his past. Yet again, and for some strange reason, the boss of the UVF's internal security department, Mr V, knows nothing about Haddock's cosy arrangement with Terry Fairfield. Mr V has never uncovered an informant, just like his chief of staff.

Haddock seemed to go from one extreme to another. One minute he was protecting an informant and his friend from being killed by the UVF; the next minute he was killing innocent Catholics. It would seem he did what he liked depending on his mood on a particular day. All down the years when I was making sure his name was never out of the media and the public eye, he was constantly conspiring to kill me either by himself personally or using his Mount Vernon cronies. But unknown to him, some of his own team were actually informing their handlers about him, and on more than one occasion these informers saved my life. On one occasion they planned to kill me by placing a bomb under my car. As well as that, I was warned that Haddock was going to kill me, but that didn't deter me and to defy him I would sit in my car outside his house in Mount Vernon. And he knew that. I wasn't afraid of him, but I had to be careful so as not to get trapped inside the estate.

Haddock was well armed and had three guns at his personal disposal: one he kept in his house at all times which was only removed when his handlers warned him that his house was going to be searched. He was always given enough advance warning to make sure the gun was off the premises when the police raiding party came knocking. The two other guns were kept in UVF arms dumps in the estate. The pub I drank in was visited many times by people sent by Haddock to see if it was possible to kill me either inside or when I left. On one occasion he sent a man and a woman into the pub as a courting couple out socialising for an evening. Haddock thought he was being clever using this couple as his scouts, but his cleverness was to be his downfall. I knew he was rattled, and he knew that if he didn't kill me then more of his dark and dirty secrets would be splashed across the media, in particular the Sunday papers. I knew he didn't like that. Fortunately for me Haddock hadn't the guts to come after me and shoot me dead. He would have enjoyed that in some sick way. He told some of his cronies that his ultimate fantasy was to watch someone being beaten to death. How warped and sick can an individual stoop in life?

Throughout Haddock's reign of terror, he had more than his Special Branch and CID handlers looking out for him. His boss, Rab Warnock, another convicted UVF man who was exposed many times in the *Sunday World* as a long-standing police informant, turned a blind eye to Haddock's activities so long as the money from drug dealing, racketeering, prostitution and taxi firms kept rolling in on a weekly basis. Money literally bought his silence. To this day I wonder how Warnock sleeps at night or what he sees when he looks in the mirror in the morning. He is another individual I wouldn't mind meeting on a dark night just to let him know my feelings. Warnock must have thought Haddock was the perfect terrorist, given the number of murders chalked up for the UVF in north Belfast, yet no UVF men were caught or charged. When I look at who Warnock appointed as his provost marshall many years ago, I wonder was it his choice or was it that of the Special Branch. The person he appointed was also a Special Branch informant from Monkstown, a man who had briefly worked with me as a doorman. He has done quite well for himself and now owns a taxi firm despite his criminal career which included a period in jail after he and several others were caught carrying out a robbery on a house in another part of Belfast. When this informant was sacked as a doorman, he sent a 'team' to the bar where he had previously worked to 'do me'. They didn't succeed and as a result his ego was hugely deflated.

Haddock, as it turned out, was the power behind Warnock, and Warnock knew that. He protected Haddock at all costs and lied to the UVF leadership. When Haddock and his men killed Presbyterian minister Reverend David Templeton in his Newtownabbey home, Warnock did nothing. Haddock and his team wrongly believed Templeton was a paedophile, when in fact he was gay. They gave the minister a terrible beating that night when they broke into his home, but he survived long enough to name Haddock as his main attacker to a member of his medical staff before he died. I spoke to that medical staff member who confirmed to me what Templeton said: Haddock was the main assailant. Was Haddock ever charged with this brutal assault and murder. The answer again is no.

The critics of the O'Loan report have repeatedly pointed out how well the Special Branch have behaved and how many lives they have saved, but I have to point out that Mark Haddock is linked to more murders when the Special Branch took over complete control of him than when the CID were running him on their own or even jointly with the Special Branch. For example, when Haddock's car was searched and a piece of paper was found which had an address and car registration following the murder of Tommy English in 2000, he told the police after his arrest that someone had given him the document and that it was not his handwriting. He also told them that in the past he had provided a police officer with details of cars acting suspiciously in his area and added that he thought he may have asked this officer to do a check on the vehicle. The officer he referred to stated that at no time did Haddock ask him to do a vehicle registration check on the car. Haddock was charged with possession of information likely to be of use to terrorists. It was another glorious opportunity to take Haddock off the streets for good, but his senior Special Branch handler, a detective sergeant, prepared a confidential document to be forwarded to the DPP. It was a favourable account of Haddock's history as an informant and stated: 'The recent arrest was due to unavoidable and unfortunate circumstances which were not under his control. There were no sinister motives behind the possession of the vehicle registration number and I am of the opinion that he will be of great value in the future and he is aware that there were unavoidable circumstances which have resulted in his present circumstances.' The DPP issued a direction of 'No prosecution' on the charge and Haddock was in the clear again. If that detective sergeant's report is not misleading, I don't know what is.

Here the police had a known UVF commander caught with the address and car registration number of a man who had just been murdered. The detective sergeant failed to mention in his confidential report that the reason why Haddock had been stopped and arrested was not just because he was the main suspect in the Tommy English murder, but he was also in charge and in control of the UVF team which carried out the murder as part of a feud that year with the UDA. In my humble opinion the Special Branch colluded in a cover-up of the Tommy English murder. It is the only conclusion any right-thinking person could come to, looking at all these facts.

Haddock had lived a charmed life with the help of the Special Branch, but when his PSNI agent status was removed in 2003 following a review, he was now out on his own. Time was running out for him, and following his arrest for the attempted murder of Trevor Gowdy, he had few friends in jail. The UVF cut his welfare payments and he became *persona non grata* on UVF landings in Maghaberry Prison. He had to be housed in a safe block in the jail and it was at this point that he made one final attempt to join the Loyalist Volunteer Force (LVF). He was told to get lost. His only other friend in the safe compound was another UVF tout, 'supergrass' Clifford McKeown. I would love to have been a fly on the wall when those two were having their private conversations. Outside the concrete walls and 30 ft high security fencing of his new home in Maghaberry, time was slowly but surely running out for agent Roxy. It was only a matter of time before all would be revealed about him. Thank God, I used to say. Thank God. All my efforts were not in vain. As he carried out his last act as a UVF man during the Gowdy trial, Haddock was starting to show the strain; he was a man under pressure. The trial judge decided to release him on bail, despite police objections regarding his safety. Trevor Gowdy had taken ill on the stand and needed some months to recover. The coward that he is, Haddock left the court along with 'Judas' Moore with his coat jacket pulled up over his face to hide his identity.

But I knew what he looked like and I had received information about where he would be living while on bail. A reliable source told me he was living beside the Templeton Hotel in Templepatrick, Co. Antrim, and it was just a twenty minute drive north out of Belfast. He and his girlfriend Helen McAllister were staying in a luxury apartment down a narrow lane off the main road in Templepatrick. At 6 o'clock the next morning I was sitting in a car outside his apartment which was in complete darkness. It appeared there was no one at home, but I had spotted his girlfriend's car which was parked close to the exit. This I hoped was my chance to have that yarn with the scumbag who had our lovely son murdered. But I sensed something wasn't right. I had a feeling that this opportunity to get up close and personal to my son's killer had come about too easily. For some reason there wasn't a light on anywhere. I told the man driving the car to get out of Templepatrick and make it quick.

It is my belief that the source who had given me the information had unwittingly been given the chance to set me up to be arrested by the police. I think it was the police's belief that I would kill Haddock with the result that nothing would be revealed about him and I would be either shot or sent to prison. But I had been around too many corners before and I wasn't going to fall into such a carefully laid trap, no matter how enticing the bait was.

In the end it didn't really matter because the UVF shot Haddock themselves in what can only be described as a botched operation using a .22 calibre weapon. I wondered if it was a serious attempt to kill him, given the weapon involved, because if they really wanted him dead they could have put their hands on a shotgun quite easily and blown his head off. He survived and became a drain on the public purse having to spend weeks in the intensive care unit at the Royal Victoria Hospital in Belfast under armed police guard. Agent Roxy recovered sufficiently to be put in an isolation wing of Maghaberry Prison away from other UVF prisoners who would be under orders to kill him at any given opportunity. But he lives a lonely existence with no real friends to watch over him. He can't trust anyone and when he is finally released he will spend the rest of his days waiting for that bullet. I hope he suffers mentally because of the misery and heartache he has caused so many people.

What is more important to me is that young Raymond knows I kept my word to him and exposed Haddock for what he was and what he had done. He ordered the murder of a son I dearly loved and miss. But I am not finished and I will not rest until the killers are dealt with. I made that solemn promise to young Raymond's mum, and it is a promise I intend to keep, so help me God.

13.
Hitting the Election Trail

I had never any real thoughts of putting my name forward to seek election to the Stormont Assembly in March 2007. All my time had been taken up with the Police Ombudsman's report on Raymond's murder. Other victims' relatives were in contact with me to discuss the report and how it impacted on their lives. It was a hectic time and my body was aching from back pain. I sat down with Vivienne and my sons to discuss how we could take forward our campaign for justice for Raymond.

What changed my mind to run as a candidate was an appearance on Friday, 26 January, by the DUP's Jeffrey Donaldson MP on BBC television to be interviewed about the O'Loan report. Instead of condemning police misconduct, he attempted to condemn my role as a parent and asked why I did not report my son to the RUC for being a member of the UVF. I couldn't believe my ears that a man who once promised to name my son's UVF killers in the House of Commons was now vilifying me. The victims didn't matter, only the good name of the RUC.

What started off with me asking Donaldson why he had

made those remarks became a very heated discussion. Mr Donaldson reminded me that when I was criticising him and other Unionist politicians, I did not have a mandate. A mandate for what? My son was murdered and a respectable team of experienced investigators had just exposed paid police informants who were murdering people. And Donaldson said I had no mandate. I went to bed with his cheap shot ringing in my ears: 'You don't have a mandate.' I thought, I am going to make Mr Donaldson eat his words.

After Donaldson's unwarranted outburst against me, I decided to stand in the Assembly elections and spread the message that collusion happened in both communities. There was much work to be done: posters, election pamphlets, and money to pay for it all. The posters were to be simple: a photo of me with my slogan, 'Vote McCord, for Truth and Justice, Proper Policing and an end to paramilitary gangsterism.' I also drew up an election manifesto with the help of my old friend Mark Langhammer, a councillor and an experienced trade unionist. Part of my manifesto read: 'During the past ten years I have had to fight for justice with no real help particularly from Unionist politicians. A few weeks ago my campaign was vindicated in a devastating report by the Police Ombudsman. . . . The Truth came out . . . Justice and Truth for everyone, not selective justice. If elected, the promise I give is to speak and fight for all the people. . . . Working-class areas across north Belfast are scourged by paramilitary control. . . . The price has seen police turn a blind eye to the drug dealing, criminality, racketeering and gangsterism of paramilitaries across north Belfast.'

As the election drew near, I was able to draw on the help of a Catholic family from west Belfast whom I had never met, just spoken to on the phone. They too had a close relative murdered by thugs in their own community and asked me if I needed any help with my election. We arranged to meet the following night on the New Lodge Road to go door to door and hand out my election leaflets. Two cars drew up outside a pub in the New Lodge Road and five women got out. At last I could put a face to the voice on the phone. These women had nothing to gain from me. All they wanted to do was help a father seeking truth and justice. As we stood talking, a fire tender pulled up and a couple of firemen got out, shook my hand, wished me all the best and told me to keep fighting for Raymond. It was very encouraging and incidents like that happened more and more, with ordinary people approaching me and urging me to keep battling on. After the firemen left us, the women took the election leaflets and off they went. It was absolutely fantastic. They were typical Belfast women, hard on the outside with a soft centre. The five women were among many who wanted to help, like my poster designer who didn't charge me anything for his work; the printers who ran off my posters for free; and there were the working-class people of north Belfast who helped out financially. My campaign was gathering momentum, but we soon realised we needed more posters to cover the whole of the constituency. No part of north Belfast was without a Raymond McCord election poster — from Catholic Ardoyne to Protestant Rathcoole. How many of the other candidates could say they crossed the divide? Very few.

I started canvassing in Rathcoole where the UDA had tried to kill me. I stood outside the main shops facing their drinking club. Mark Langhammer joined me talking to passersby, many I hadn't seen for years. A couple of newspaper photographers witnessed me standing in an estate where the UDA told me I would be shot on my return. Not too many UDA bosses came out to order me out of the estate.

No one shunned me. In fact the opposite was the case. But there was concern when word filtered out to the paramilitaries. I was at the Diamond shops canvassing when a carload of paramilitary wannabes drove up. One big lad got out and swaggered towards me. For a split second I thought about stopping the canvassing and teaching this 'tough guy' the finer art of street fighting. But the closer he got, the bravado left him and he turned round and went back to his car. I had proved my point to the paramilitary bully boys.

We then headed to the Catholic Bawnmore estate, five minutes from Rathcoole. I actually felt safer in Bawnmore and Mark was well known to many residents. We parked his car in the heart of the estate and at the first door we knocked, Mark explained who I was and what we were doing. The man's wife came out and said they had just been talking about me. She assured me I could count on their votes. This is the start of my mandate, Mr Donaldson, I said to myself. That day I was treated with courtesy by the residents of Bawnmore who made us feel very welcome — so much so that we spent more time in Bawnmore than we did in Rathcoole. We bumped into a Sinn Féin election worker, a man I had known from years back. A photographer snapped us shaking hands with the Sinn Féin election worker and he told me privately that he was going to vote for me. As we said goodbye, a woman who was walking behind us playing with her son said in front of the Sinn Féin man that she would be voting for me. Mark and I walked to another house where to our surprise the owner knew both of us and invited us in for a cup of tea and a bowl of home-made vegetable soup which I declined. He and his friend offered to put up my election posters. When I asked the house owner how many he wanted, he replied, 'As many as you want to give me.' We discussed the Police Ombudsman's report and we agreed on justice matters, that the police had been colluding with paramilitary killers on both sides of the community. We agreed too that the State had done its best to cover up the murders, but through time they would be exposed and the truth would come out. After a lengthy discussion on the report, Mark and I left, telling the men they would have the posters within the next few days. I was really starting to get into the election. Within a few days the posters were delivered to Bawnmore and they were soon flying high on lamp-posts. I can't thank these men enough for what they did.

The poster campaign was gathering pace each day, but we had to make another order from the printers because in some loyalist areas they were cut down. I have to pay credit to one of my election helpers, Kathy, who mobilised her team day and night to put them up again. She was fearless in her support for me, as was her entire family. On the streets I was receiving fantastic public support. People driving past would toot their car horns in support; others would cross the street, shake my hand and give me solid words of encouragement. It boosted my team's morale to keep pushing on.

One evening my friend Tommy and I were putting posters up along the Antrim Road when we noticed that the only posters flying outside the Sinn Féin election office were those of its candidate, Gerry Kelly. I decided that had to change. As I was putting up the posters I noticed people looking out of the Sinn Féin office. I didn't know who they were, but they gave me the thumbs up sign and waved at me. I laughed out loud and waved back. Twenty years ago this would never have happened. As we worked our way up the New Lodge Road, a pensioner came over to Tommy and me to complain about a group of teenagers drinking at the side of her house. She told us about the empty drink cans and rubbish they were leaving behind, cluttering up the side of her house. The woman said they also urinated in the street and no one was doing anything to stop it. On several occasions she had gone to the local Sinn Féin centre to complain, and still nothing was being done. She thought we were two Sinn Féin election workers from the centre! When she realised her mistake, she took a good look at me and said: 'You're that man McCord, aren't you?' I said I was, whereupon she shook my hand and asked me where I had lived as a child. I pointed over to the park across the road at the bottom of the New Lodge Road and said I was born in a street which had long been demolished. The woman asked me which McCord my mother was and I said Kathleen. It turned out she and mum had worked together in one of the mills in York Street sixty years ago. I told my mother, who is now aged 80, the next day about who I met and it just showed how small the city really is. To this day I still don't know if the woman voted for me!

We had several other interesting incidents on the New Lodge Road. On one occasion a group of men came out of one of the pubs and watched us erecting posters facing their bar. A couple of them came over to enquire who the posters were for, and I said they were for me. The response was incredible. They all gave me a handshake, told me to keep going and said: 'Your son would be proud of you.' It was another special moment but one I was getting everywhere I went. The response from people in Catholic and Protestant areas of north Belfast was very warm and friendly, except for the few dirty looks I received from some paramilitary figures.

After a good response to our electioneering in Rathcoole, I decided to go back and put up some posters at the Diamond shops where nearly everybody on the estate would see them. My friend Tommy, a Catholic, accompanied me there one night. Tommy had no fear in him and it made no difference to him whether it was Rathcoole or Ardoyne. Just as in Bawnmore and in the Ardoyne, the people in Rathcoole came up and talked to us about the election. Other men I knew in Rathcoole helped put up posters for me and not one was ever pulled down. The tide was slowly turning in an estate where at one time people would have been too frightened to talk to me. Now, not only were people coming over to speak to me, but they also wanted to help me. In a short period of time my election poster was hanging from many lamp-posts in Rathcoole. The people could see my face when they went into the estate, when they went to buy their groceries at the Diamond and when they went to cast their votes at the polling stations. One day a UVF man drove past tooting his horn and waving at me. Changed times, I thought. But I was no goat's toe and I watched every car going past because if the UVF or the UDA were going to attack me, they would need to be quick and send someone who had more than just a drop of bravado.

With Rathcoole finished, we decided to take my election message on to the Shore Road and Mount Vernon areas in north Belfast. It was going to be dangerous because the UVF were intent on killing me and they knew the only way they could do it would be through some cowardly act like shooting me from behind. For all their macho image, they didn't have the stomach to face me on their own without a gun or a baseball bat. I was concerned about the possibility of a gunman or a passing car as the posters had to be erected at night. I would love to have seen their faces when they drove along the main road outside Mount Vernon or past their drinking dens the following morning. In Mount Vernon, just inside the entrance, painted on a gable wall in big white letters was the message, 'Vote McCord No. 1.' The same slogan appeared along the Shore Road and York Road and someone even painted it on the walls of a local UVF bar.

I later found out who it was, and shook the hand of a very brave man.

Life was now changing for the bully boys because posters and slogans in support of me were going up in territory controlled by the UVF. I also put up posters along another part of York Road which was UDA territory, but I knew I would face no problems from that organisation in that district. The reason was the UDA in Tigers Bay hated Mount Vernon UVF almost as much as I did. Another reason was the UDA in Tigers Bay were not the same as Rathcoole UDA and held no bitterness towards me. In fact their members actually went out of their way to be friendly towards me. I had never caused them any problems, so they left me alone.

My poster campaign was nearing an end and the only area left was the Ardoyne district, both the Catholic and Protestant sides of it. We decided to go out on a Saturday morning and we walked the Catholic streets of Ardoyne. I was given a warm welcome. One man approached me, said hello and asked how we were doing. When I told him we were putting up election posters, he said I would have no problems in the area. I took it from the way he was talking that he spoke with some authority and was probably a local republican, a Sinn Féin man. He told me who he was and I had guessed right. After a brief conversation outside a shop, a little old lady came up to me and told me she was going to vote for me but said she had to wait until the 'Shinner' had gone away before she approached me. Over on the Protestant side of Ardoyne, a couple I knew, John and Carol, invited me into their home to have a cup of tea with them. Both of them are real diamonds as far as I am concerned, old friends who typified Belfast people, kindness personified. I didn't have any problems in the Protestant side of the Ardoyne and when we had finished in that area, the electioneering was nearly over. Election day was upon us.

As the polling booths opened on Thursday, 7 March 2007, some of my supporters went to the polling stations to hand out leaflets as the voters came in. I visited as many of them as I possibly could. No one was ignorant towards me even if they were not going to vote for me. But that didn't stop some of the election workers being confrontational. Some of the DUP workers at a polling station on the edge of Rathcoole decided to try and dictate to one of my supporters where and how he could hand out the leaflets. They picked on the wrong man, my son Gareth, trying to lay down 'election law'. Gareth would stand up and fight his corner with anyone, just like my other son Glenn. The DUP workers included a local councillor who should have known better as he, like myself, was originally from York Street and he also knew my mother and father. When he told Gareth that I was helping Sinn Féin by running against the DUP and that my actions might cost the DUP a seat, Gareth was totally taken aback by his arrogance. Just who the hell did this man think he was, I thought. Why should I stand aside for a party that had failed unionist victims? I was very proud of Gareth that day because he handled the situation extremely well and I believe the DUP councillor and his group lost the argument. Later that evening at another polling station, Gareth crossed swords with the DUP's North Belfast MP, Nigel Dodds. But to the credit of both, they shook hands and left on friendly terms. Gareth just likes to get his point across and I admire that. These people at the polling stations seemed to have forgotten that he had lost his older brother and all he was doing was helping his father get justice for him. My other son Glenn was also at the forefront of my election campaign. Along with some of his friends, he helped to put up my election posters. He is nobody's fool and would go through fire for his family. By 10 o'clock that night the voting was over. Now we had to wait for the counting to start.

The following morning, a few of my election team and some supporters decided to meet in Belfast city centre before being taken by car to the King's Hall in south Belfast where the counting would begin for the four areas of Belfast — North, South, East and West. Among them were John, Frank (who thinks he can sing better than me!), Tommy and Kathy. It was a day to remember and it was an amazing experience walking about and rubbing shoulders with some of the province's leading politicians. But as we waited for the first results to come in, I found myself in a row with the DUP again. I locked horns with Jimmy Spratt, who was standing for South Belfast for the DUP, over the Police Ombudsman's report. This is the same Jimmy Spratt who is the former chairman of the Police Federation which represented rank-and-file members of the RUC/PSNI. The report obviously didn't go down too well with him because it criticised officers who were members of the Police Federation. I took grave offence at some of the comments he made. All I can say is that he is a very fortunate man because if it hadn't been for the fact that there were so many people about and the fact that my supporters stepped in to intervene, I would not have been responsible for my actions. He made my blood boil that day, but it was typical of Unionist politicians who just love to shoot the messenger and ignore the message.

When the first results came in, Nigel Dodds was duly elected to the Assembly to represent North Belfast again. I walked over to him, shook his hand and congratulated him on the result. In fairness to Nigel, he was friendly and spoke to me about the events of the night before with Gareth. Nigel made promises to both Gareth and me which I can't divulge, but I'm hoping he keeps to them. I did the same when Gerry

Kelly of Sinn Féin was elected. With the two main favourites out of the way, we watched where the ballot papers were being placed after they were counted. My box was building steadily. All around the hall there were many long and worried-looking faces, particularly among the Ulster Unionist Party candidates. They had taken a hammering in the Westminster elections and now had only one MP, the lovely Lady Sylvia Hermon, representing the party in the House of Commons. As the Assembly elections were later to show, it was another disaster for the UUP. I spoke to many candidates that day and none were more friendly than those from Sinn Féin, including their party leader Gerry Adams. I may disagree with his hope for a United Ireland, but the man has always been civil and courteous towards me, unlike some of the Unionist politicians I had met.

When the final result came in, my supporters and I were not disappointed. The votes were counted under a system called proportional representation (PR), instead of first past the post. Like myself, my friend Tommy was confused as to how the system worked. Tommy was such a character that day. He kept going over to Gerry Kelly and telling him, now that he was elected he should give his surplus to me. Kelly kept saying yes, but Tommy didn't understand that Kelly had no say in where his surplus would go. The counters sorted all that out. Tommy made us smile, laugh and cry because all he was doing was trying to get me as many votes as possible. As the day progressed and different candidates were eliminated, I was still hanging on, much to the disgust of some politicians, particularly within the DUP. Out of the race were the Alliance Party, the Workers' Party, the Green Party and also Robert McCartney's UK Unionist Party. My first preference votes had been counted. I had polled a very respectable 1,320 votes, 4.4 per cent of the total votes cast.

Contrary to what Jeffrey Donaldson had once said, now I had an electoral mandate. One thousand, three hundred and twenty people in north Belfast believed in me by giving me their first preference vote. How many DUP candidates would have been elected if they had stood as independents? Not many, I think. The DUP only had to look at how one of the party's one-time golden boys, Paul Berry, did when he stood as an independent and failed to get re-elected. This count mattered a lot to me and even though I didn't get elected on the PR system, I live to fight another day. The people of north Belfast had put their faith in me and I hope I didn't disappoint them.

We left the King's Hall that night and Kathy dropped us off in Belfast city centre at a pub for some refreshments. We had a great night. After a few beers Frank thought he could sing my favourite song, 'King of the Road', better than me. But after hearing his version, not for the first time, I jokingly told him he needed more practice if he wanted to come up to my standard! In fact, I'm the worst singer in Belfast.

I went home that night a happy man. A father who had lost a wonderful son to paid police informants now had a political mandate to carry on my fight for justice for young Raymond despite what Jeffrey Donaldson thought. When I attacked his party or challenged him to a television debate, he told me to be careful as I was now in the 'big boys' league. But I had turned the tables on him with my election result. His party's third candidate in the North Belfast constituency failed to get elected. I'm sure that candidate is eternally grateful that Donaldson made those comments because if he hadn't, I would never have stood. Some of the DUP election workers later blamed me for their candidate not getting elected. But I know who I would blame. And it is not me.

14.
Washington Hears My Story

I was left buoyant after my first foray into the election battlefield with so many people in north Belfast giving me their first preference vote. They had given me a platform to build on and I was not prepared to leave the public stage just because I had upset some Unionist politicians.

I was also determined not to slip away from the public spotlight because I wanted to keep the Police Ombudsman's report high on the political agenda. I had come too far to prove my complaints that RUC/PSNI officers had colluded with UVF murder gangs in north Belfast just to drop off the political radar screen. But I don't believe north Belfast was an isolated case, because from what I have been told the Special Branch doesn't operate like that.

One day I received a phone call from Mark Thompson, the director of Relatives for Justice, which is based on the Falls Road in west Belfast. Mark asked me if I would be prepared to go to Washington to speak about young Raymond's case. I met Mark several times, and Clara Reilly, another member of Relatives for Justice, and they made me feel very welcome. I told my story and I listened to the others recalling how they had lost a loved one. We then formulated a plan to bring the issue of collusion to a wider audience and push for justice. No such group existed within the Protestant community, probably because Protestants like myself believed that collusion was just republican propaganda. I had practically fought on my own for justice for my son because I was getting little support in my own backyard. The UVF leadership and its late political master David Ervine did absolutely nothing to help my family. They told lies, peddled misinformation, made false promises and covered up for a gang of murdering touts. I accepted Mark's invitation as it was a glorious opportunity for me to speak to the most powerful politicians on Capitol Hill. For years the powerful Irish-American lobby championed the cause of the nationalist community. Now they were going to hear the story of a unionist father and I would offer them the chance to support me. I had no better weapon in my armoury than the Police Ombudsman's report which had highlighted one of the Irish-American lobby's most talked about subjects, collusion.

We left Belfast by coach for Dublin Airport at 5 a.m. on Monday, 12 March, to catch our transatlantic flight. Travelling with me were other relatives who had lost loved ones through collusion: Theresa Slane whose husband Gerard was shot dead by the UFF in west Belfast in September 1988; Paul McIlwaine whose son David was savagely murdered by the UVF's Mid-Ulster brigade in February 2000; Pauline Davey-Kennedy whose Sinn Féin councillor father John was shot dead by the UVF in February 1989; Clara Reilly whose brother Jim Burns was murdered by the UVF in February 1981; and Relatives for Justice director Mark Thompson whose brother Peter was shot dead by the British Army in January 1990 during a robbery at a west Belfast bookies shop.

When we touched down in Washington we were totally exhausted. I was shattered as I had been up since 4 a.m. and still had lower back pain. I shared a room with Paul McIlwaine and Mark Thompson. Our night's sleep was shattered by the sound of Paul's snoring. It sounded like the Blitz; how his wife Gail slept in the same room is beyond me. But as Paul is a devoted Christian, I couldn't use the language I wanted to even if he deserved it.

Our first meeting on Tuesday, 13 March, was inside Capitol Building. There were armed police everywhere just to make us feel at home. The briefing took place in room H-137 with the Congressional Friends of Ireland, a powerful lobby group that could influence those in the corridors of power on Capitol Hill. Congressmen, senators and people interested in hearing our personal stories had turned out in force. A reporter and a photographer from the *Sunday World* had travelled over on a separate flight to cover my trip at my request because I wanted the people back in Northern Ireland to know exactly what was being said in Washington.

Each of us — Theresa, Pauline, Clara, myself and Paul — spoke for a few minutes about our cases and how the security forces had colluded with loyalist paramilitaries. It was the first time American politicians were to hear of police collusion in Protestant murders. The Americans were getting their eyes opened and were starting to get the picture that the forces of law and order would do anything except tell the truth. There would have been no shame in showing emotion that morning. It is a macho thing not to cry, but when your heart is breaking for a son so cruelly taken from you, it is hard to be in full control of your emotions all the time. The politicians and other dignitaries in the room who had heard similar accusations in the past from the nationalist/republican side were now hearing it from two Protestant fathers, which I think made a big difference. This was breaking new ground for Paul and me because we were delivering our personal tragedies to an audience who had long been told that the security forces had colluded with loyalists to kill nationalists and republicans.

Every politician at the first meeting promised to raise Raymond's case at the highest level in Washington. They just couldn't understand how some politicians wanted to attack Mrs O'Loan and her office rather than call for the corrupt police officers and UVF killers to be brought to justice. Congressman Ritchie Neal said he had had 'grave concerns' for a number of years about collusion between the police and loyalist paramilitaries. Now he had the proof to support those concerns. Congressman Chris Smith added: 'Mrs O'Loan has done a tremendous job in getting to the bottom of a complex issue.' He vowed to help all the families in their search for truth and justice. I had to pinch myself many times as I was rubbing shoulders with some of the world's most influential people. But each day I was driving home my message loud and clear: The RUC/PSNI had colluded with loyalist killer gangs to murder a young Protestant man.

By the time our week was over in Washington and New York, American politicians were left in no doubt about the 'dirty war' involving the RUC/PSNI and the UVF. Orla O'Hanrahan, the political counsellor at the Irish Embassy in Washington, opened her door to me. She listened intently and promised to give whatever help she could. Her support and that of others was in stark contrast to how I had been treated back home by Unionist politicians. I was asked many times on the trip what the Unionist politicians were doing for the victims. Nothing.

We started the second day of our east coast trip with an early breakfast meeting with Paula Dobriansky, an under-secretary at the US State Department, a powerful woman on Capitol Hill when it came to Irish affairs. I had been informed that I was going to meet President George W. Bush that week. I could hardly believe that a man like me from the back streets of York Street in north Belfast was now going to the White House to meet the most powerful man in the world. It was a totally unbelievable experience.

I thanked Paula for her kind invitation, but I seized the moment to raise the case of a man I had met the day before, who had set up home in New York but who was originally from the Lower Ormeau/Markets district of south Belfast. He was a Catholic and until I had arrived in Washington I had never met him. Malachy McAllister is a former republican prisoner who for many years had been fighting deportation from the US back to Belfast. Malachy fled Belfast in 1988 with his wife Bernadette and their four children when the UFF shot up their Lower Ormeau Road home. No one was injured when gunmen raked his house with automatic gunfire. Malachy and his family first fled to Canada, then crossed the border into the US before finally settling in New Jersey. Since then he had been fighting deportation as an illegal immigrant. I asked Paula Dobriansky to look into Malachy's case to see if she could help him to stay in America because if he was sent back to Belfast, loyalist paramilitaries would try to kill him. Paula gave me an undertaking that she would do something positive for Malachy and his family. I showed her a framed photograph of Raymond in his RAF uniform. I wanted her to see just how young and how handsome he was, and to know that I had lost a treasured son. She promised to do whatever she could in my quest for justice.

During the trip Raymond's picture was never far from my side, my guardian angel. I was carrying him around under my arm when I met the reporter and photographer from the *Sunday World* on the steps of Capitol Hill. I clutched him between my two hands as I was proud to show him off, and I remember saying to myself, this is for you, Raymond.

From 9 a.m. until sometimes 8.30 p.m. we had a succession of important meetings in various buildings on Capitol Hill. On one of the days our group was going to a meeting in the Senate building when I was informed that Dawn Purvis, the newly elected leader of the PUP, was in Senator Ted Kennedy's office. I left my friends and hurried to the senator's office where several of Senator Kennedy's office staff were at their desks. When I asked if Dawn Purvis had been in, they said she had. This was a disgrace, that a senator of Ted Kennedy's huge political standing would want to speak to the leader of the UVF's political wing. How could any democratic person want to speak to someone who is an apologist for the UVF? Senator Kennedy's staff listened and I asked them, 'How would you like it if the political leader of an Arab terrorist group like Al Qa'eda entered Capitol Hill for a meeting?' I am not saying Dawn Purvis is a terrorist, but her predecessor, the late David Ervine, was once quoted as saying that he had been 'headhunted by the UVF' to run the PUP. And I know he took his political direction from the head of the UVF, John 'Bunter' Graham, another security force informant. Thankfully, Senator Kennedy's staff saw my point of view and a meeting was arranged for our group to meet a very senior member of his staff. The meeting was held the following day as well as a separate meeting in the office of Senator John McCain. Both meetings gave everyone the opportunity to urge these powerful politicians to put the British government under pressure to do something positive for all the victims.

Our trip coincided with the most important date on the

Irish American calendar, St Patrick's Day. We were all invited to the Irish Ambassador's residence in Washington for a St Patrick's night reception two days before the big parade. Ambassador David Connolly and his wife Christine, lovely, down to earth people, had thrown open the doors to their beautiful home. It was a night to remember and, to be honest, I thought I had walked through the wrong door and into a stand-up comedy show. The man providing the entertainment was none other than the Taoiseach himself, Bertie Ahern. If he ever decided to leave politics he could always get himself a slot as a comedian. Believe me, Bertie was very good and he had the 500 invited guests in stitches. Bertie was certainly 'King of the Hill' that night with his five-star performance. Bertie has a common touch and can mix with the great, the good and the working class. As I stood in the downstairs drawing room sipping on a glass of Guinness, Irish Foreign Affairs Minister Dermot Ahern approached me and shook my hand. I had never met him before in my life, but you would have thought he had known me for years, such was his warmth. He told me there was someone in the next room who wanted to meet me. I went in and a small man came forward from the packed crowd and greeted me with a warm and firm handshake. It was the 'King of the Hill' himself, Bertie Ahern. 'Are my people looking after you, Raymond?' he asked. 'They are,' was all I could say, gently slapping him on his belly. We stood for a few minutes and had a general chat and I was promised another meeting with him in Dublin. It was a very positive moment in my family's campaign.

Other guests that night included the McCartney sisters whose brother Robert was murdered by IRA men. They too were hoping for help from the Americans. Unionist, Nationalist and Republican politicians had also gathered in the ambassador's residence, but there was no fighting over religion or politics. I also met the Sinn Féin MP Martin McGuinness, now the Assembly's deputy first minister. I found him very pleasant and courteous. As we stood chatting about my case, a few people came forward and asked if they could take a picture of us with their guests. I still have that photo and it shows me with my fist firmly planted underneath Martin's jaw. It was all in good humour.

It had been a worthwhile night out, but we had to leave because I had a busy day ahead of me. The following morning I was up early to get prepared for the reception with President Bush at the White House. I hadn't a clue what to expect, but I heard that controversy was raging behind the scenes. I was told that British officials were doing their best to make sure there was no invitation for me. Unfortunately for them, their diplomatic overtures fell on deaf ears. My invitation stood and I am sure certain figures within the British government and the Northern Ireland Office were left red-faced.

I was standing in the rain at the gates of the White House when I met Geraldine Finucane, the widow of solicitor Pat Finucane, and her son John. Geraldine explained to me what it was like inside and gave me an insight into what would happen. I walked in with them through the tight security where you had to identify yourself and have your credentials checked before the burly Secret Service agents let you in. On the way in I bumped into Fr Sean McManus who had founded the very influential Washington-based lobby group, the Irish National Caucus. I had met him on Capitol Hill on my first day and a few nights later he took Paul McIlwaine and me out to dinner to a very fancy restaurant. It had a reputation in Washington for its steaks and that suited Paul and me because Fr Sean wanted to take us to either a

Chinese, Italian or Thai restaurant, but I stepped in and told him: 'I'm a meat and potatoes man.' He was slightly taken aback and couldn't believe we had turned down a nice meal in one of these restaurants. We ended up in an up-market restaurant that night and it was a dining experience Fr Sean was never to forget. A waitress presented us with a menu but the only thing on my mind was a big, thick, well-done steak, much to the horror of Fr Sean. I don't like blood running out of meat on my plate, but Fr Sean guided me on a road to a Damascus conversion that night and convinced me to eat it medium. The waitress then asked me what sauce I would like and I said gravy, because it was the only way I ate steak at home. The waitress glared at me as if I had just sprouted horns. Fr Sean almost fell off his seat in shock.

After getting our security clearance, we walked into the White House and Fr Sean told me to stay close to him as he would introduce me to several prominent people. I told them about young Raymond's murder and the extent of the collusion. They were amazed at what they were being told about Northern Ireland. We were then escorted into a large room where the entertainment was to be held. Everyone knew exactly where they were to sit. No sooner had we been seated when George W. Bush and Bertie Ahern entered the room and stood together on the stage. The annual handing over of a large spray of shamrock from Bertie to the President took place before Mr Bush made a short speech. Then the entertainment started and the night was in full swing with a fabulous group of singers.

We left the White House almost as swiftly as we arrived and we were ushered outside to where a special bus was waiting to take a group of us to another reception. This time I was heading to the British Embassy on Massachusetts Avenue. Taking a seat at the front of the bus, an American politician sat down beside me wearing cowboy boots. He asked me where I was from and I told him my background. I explained about Raymond and the cover-up and collusion after his murder. The American, who actually had a striking resemblance to John Wayne, was astounded. I used the opportunity to tell him about the lack of support from the PUP in getting justice for young Raymond and when I explained to him that the new leader of the PUP was in town for the St Patrick's Day celebrations, he didn't look a bit pleased. And neither did the person in the seat behind me who I made sure heard every word of our conversation, Dawn Purvis of the PUP. She never said a word. To be truthful there wasn't much she could say because what I had told the American was the truth.

The British Embassy lunch was splendid and after the ambassador's speech, the Northern Ireland Secretary Peter Hain, who was seated only yards away from my table and two seats away from Dawn Purvis, spoke for a few minutes. He praised everyone he could think of, even me. He said I was a brave father fighting for justice. As his words echoed around the room, I wondered had he forgotten about the day he nodded off three times during a meeting with myself and Lady Sylvia Hermon when we were discussing my case. As soon as the speeches were over, people gathered in groups for a chat, but no one stood and talked to me except Paul McIlwaine. I hadn't come all this way to be ignored. Peter Hain, Dawn Purvis and a few others were in deep conversation together as I approached them. I handed Dawn Purvis a document and she asked me what it was. I told her that when she had time she should read it, because she would find it very interesting as it contained all the facts about the UVF murder of my son. It was a rare moment. You could have heard a pin drop among a gathering of such luminaries. I was

satisfied that I had interrupted their cosy chat and Dawn
Purvis appeared embarrassed, and not for the first time on
the trip. Just a few days before, at a breakfast appointment,
she admitted to me in front of other people that there had
been collusion in UVF murders. I am sure she must have
wanted to bite her tongue off after her statement as it backed
up everything I had been saying for years. After I dropped the
bombshell document in Dawn Purvis's hand, Paul and I left
the luncheon. It wasn't really our scene and we had a long
journey ahead — New York and the St Patrick's Day parade.

We travelled by road from Washington to New York as all
flights into the Big Apple had been cancelled because of
blizzard conditions with the result that traffic was nose-to-
tail on the interstate. I wanted to get to New York on the
Friday night to watch the 'Derry Destroyer' John Duddy fight
at the Gardens in Madison Square, but we didn't make it to
New York until the early hours of the morning.

Later that morning the streets of New York were covered
in a blanket of crunchy snow. We had breakfast and then
headed over to Fifth Avenue to watch the parade. I loved it.
The marchers and bands were dressed in green and white
and everyone was happy. There were no drunks abusing the
marchers; there were no fights; and there were no
paramilitary flags. Everyone had come to celebrate Ireland's
patron saint and make a good day of it despite the freezing
temperatures. It being St Patrick's Day, there was only one
place to go for the afternoon — the pub. All the Irish bars
were filled to capacity, with the Guinness flowing like icy
water down the Hudson River. We visited a few of them that
afternoon with everyone singing Irish songs at the top of
their voices while diners tucked into champ and sausages,
boiled spuds, boiled bacon and cabbage, and burgers and
chips. I was standing at a bar counter when a man tapped me

on the shoulder and offered to buy me a drink. I turned round and to my amazement it was Sinn Féin MLA Alex Maskey. So I have proof beyond a shadow of a doubt that Alex does buy drink, despite what others say!

A few hours later and after a few more pints of fine Guinness, I took myself off to bed for an early night's sleep. The previous twenty-four hours had left me exhausted and I was at times struggling to get through the long days with my lower back giving me grief. The next morning our group headed to Philadelphia where we were guest speakers at an Ancient Order of Hibernians (AOH) hall. Even before the meeting started, two AOH members bought me a Guinness which helped to steady my nerves. I almost felt like I was back home in Belfast as the people were so genuinely warm and friendly. All the members of our group took it in turn to tell their story. The packed hall sat in total silence, many shaking their heads in horror. Some in the audience even started to cry. There was a lot of raw emotion in the room. We thanked our hosts for their kind invitation and for taking the time to listen to us. We then adjourned downstairs for some refreshments and to have further private conversations with our hosts. Standing at the bar with me were two large American gentlemen who were not only AOH members but were also officers of the Philadelphia Police Department. It was the only time on my week-long trip to the US that I actually felt embarrassed. The walls of the hall were adorned with photographs of priests and bishops and I asked the two large policemen why they didn't have any pictures of Protestant clergymen on the walls. They just stared at me and one of them said: 'Raymond, this a Catholic organisation.' I quickly finished my pint and said my goodbyes.

As I was leaving, several AOH men came over to me and told me that as a result of the threats on my life in Belfast from the UVF, I would be more than welcome to stay in Philadelphia where I would be safe. It was a generous offer from our hosts who were decent, honest, down-to-earth people. That night, after a nice meal, it was such a relief to get to bed and catch up on some lost sleep.

We had an early start the next morning for Dulles Airport on our return leg home to Belfast via Dublin. I was looking forward to getting home to see my family. It had been a long, tiring but fruitful week in the United States. I had stayed in touch daily with Vivienne, Gareth and Glenn to let them know how my meetings had gone and how our campaign was progressing. Throughout the trip I had constantly thought about my grandchildren Dylan, Leah and Nicole, three lovely children who I hoped would not have to grow up in a troubled and dangerous land as their fathers had. There was no doubt that I had given American politicians and members of the public food for thought about how collusion had affected the lives of Protestants, and not just Catholics, nationalists and republicans as they had always believed. I had opened their eyes to a whole new side of Northern Ireland life where the police were perpetrating their dirty little war on both sides of the community. My hope when I arrived in the US was that the trip would further advance Raymond's case. I believe it did and the highest levels of the American administration will not forget the name of Raymond McCord Jnr.

Justice for young Raymond took another step closer in America. For so long my family and I had stood alone against the dark forces of the UVF and their security force bosses, but not any more. There is now a large groundswell of support at home and in America for our campaign to put those who killed young Raymond along with those police officers who protected them before a court of law.

I strongly believe that in the not too distant future some or all will have their day of reckoning, and I will be there to witness it. We will see what happens in the future. But to those who killed my son, rest assured I am not finished yet, not until the last breath leaves my body. It's not over until it's over, and until there's justice for Raymond. Nothing's surer.